# Breaking Free

## My spiritual transformation into a psychic medium

# KERRY-MARIE CALLANDER

**BALBOA**
PRESS

A DIVISION OF HAY HOUSE

Balboa Press books may be ordered through booksellers or by contacting:

Balboa Press
A Division of Hay House
1663 Liberty Drive
Bloomington, IN 47403
www.balboapress.com
1 (877) 407-4847

Because of the dynamic nature of the Internet, any web addresses or links contained in this book may have changed since publication and may no longer be valid. The views expressed in this work are solely those of the author and do not necessarily reflect the views of the publisher, and the publisher hereby disclaims any responsibility for them.

The author of this book does not dispense medical advice or prescribe the use of any technique as a form of treatment for physical, emotional, or medical problems without the advice of a physician, either directly or indirectly. The intent of the author is only to offer information of a general nature to help you in your quest for emotional and spiritual well-being. In the event you use any of the information in this book for yourself, which is your constitutional right, the author and the publisher assume no responsibility for your actions.

This book includes my personal recollections of my life story. For personal and professional reasons, and to maintain their anonymity, in some instance I have chosen to change some identifying characteristics of some of the people involved.

Front cover photo © Andre Budel
Back cover photo © Simon Llewellyn

ISBN: 978-1-5043-7514-6 (sc)
ISBN: 978-1-5043-7515-3 (e)

Print information available on the last page.

Balboa Press rev. date: 03/16/2017

# Contents

# *Foreword*

It is an honour to be asked to write the foreword for this book.

When I first met Kerry-Marie at my son's wedding in February 2008, I was curious. I had known her husband for many years and my first impression of her was of a genuine caring person with a special energy.

We seemed to click straight away and exchanged phone numbers. A few months later I decided to seek her out. I phoned, we met for coffee and have been friends ever since.

Kerry's story reveals how she developed her psychic gift of mediumship, and the experiences that made her who she is today.

She has been a stabilising influence for me and has helped me to handle situations, some life-changing. On occasion I have challenged her, arguing that 'No, that's not going to happen' or 'I don't know who that person or spirit is', to discover later on I could identify who Kerry had been telling me about, or that what she had told me through the spirit was likely to happen actually occurred. Once Kerry began travelling to the UK to the Arthur Findlay College she became more effective in allowing spirit to come through and her readings became more and more profound and accurate.

If you have purchased this book then you probably are a believer already. If you're not then this book nicely explains and clarifies many concepts that have helped me to trust.

As a psychologist and counsellor, I have referred many clients to Kerry-Marie and she has been instrumental in helping people to dig deeper and connect with loved ones.

I consider Kerry-Marie one of my closest friends. Without her guidance my life in many areas would have taken a completely different path.

Whatever your beliefs and wherever you are in your life, this book will provide much insight and inspiration.

Enjoy!

Jenny Gibson BA(Psych), MEd Psych (Hons), Dip EI, DipTchng

# Introduction

This is the personal journey of my life, which has been transformed through the power of spirit. As a medium, I have shared many experiences, and experienced the miraculous power that can occur through the wondrous gift of mediumship.

My story is of a life filled with joy and sorrow, ups and downs, love, passions and excitement, along with overcoming challenges that led to a transformation in my life. I have found peace through inner healing, and becoming a medium was a significant part of this. Leaving behind the shackles of my life has allowed me to live my life the way I know is right for me.

Through overcoming challenges, I have been able to heal and become stronger. I was able to break free so my spirit could fly, so I could fulfil my dream and work as a psychic medium (a gift I have always had but have not always been aware of). I have found out who I truly am and what I am here for. My journey is about forgiveness, courage and determination, and learning that no matter what happens in life, we can all achieve our dreams. There is a lot more to the world we live in than we can see, and I know now that our souls are eternal.

My story reveals how, through the gift of mediumship, I was not only able to heal and transform my own life but assist others too. I discovered that I had been blessed with the gift of spiritual insight, allowing me to help others to start to unfold their own spiritual, healing and psychic gifts within. It is a joy to help people to heal, release their own hurts, forgive and begin the journey of their own life feeling whole again and at peace with themselves.

This is not a story about anger, revenge, hurting others or fighting for my rights. It is my story about growing up and in later life discovering that through acceptance, forgiveness, love, courage and understanding I could live my purpose and empower others. Fun and laughter are indeed the best medicine. I broke free from restraints that held me back so I could follow my passion and life purpose to work as a psychic medium, shining a light to help people out of the darkness when their lives are clouded with grief and confusion.

Finally, my story is about healing and love, and spreading the word of spirit. I encourage you to do the same. You are not alone. Help and support is always there for you.

Blessings
Kerry-Marie

# *Be yourself*

Be yourself
Above all, let who you are
And what you believe in shine,
Through what you write, words you speak
And actions you take.
Know that you yourself
Have something to offer the world
However large or small it is.
It is yours and something you can share
Shine your light and be proud of who you are.

Kerry-Marie Callander

# Bridging two worlds

Waiting outside the conference room I can hear the MC's introduction. I'm about to demonstrate mediumship at my first ever show in Auckland, New Zealand. My legs are trembling and my heart is pounding as my friend Amanda rests her hand gently on my shoulder. 'Kerry, you're going to do just fine,' she whispers.

As I enter the room I look at the sea of about 150 faces staring back at me. Many look happy to see me, others seem unsure and a few are frowning and sceptical. My legs start to shake a little more and my heart pounds even louder. I take some deep breaths and recall the words from a TV presenter who I had spoken to earlier: 'Kerry-Marie, go to your heart, not your head. Your heart space is where you hold all your strength and power.' A warm, peaceful feeling comes over me, my strength returns and I can feel the energy of spirit all around me. I am ready to work.

To begin, I ask for the lights to be dimmed as a song is played to assist with bringing the two worlds together for my show 'Bridging the two worlds'. I know because of the power of love, there will be communication from the spirit world for people who really need it at this time.

Before long I sense the energy of a strong-minded lady, who, to me, feels like a mother to a woman in the audience. I know at once that her daughter is on the right-hand side of the room, near the front. The spirit tells me that she was a principal at a school, that she held herself upright, was intellectual and was saddened when she discovered her breast cancer. Her daughter puts up her hand. More evidence of her mum comes through and tears begin to flow, but they are tears of love, healing and comfort. The audience is mesmerized watching this young lady being comforted by the evidence I offer from her mother, who is now in the world of spirit.

Everything seems to flow as more messages come through from the spirit world for people in the audience. At one point a spirit lady in a wheelchair surrounded by cats approaches me, which takes me aback at first; however before long it is clear she is coming through to support her daughter. The facts she gives me are very accurate so her daughter knows it is her mum that is speaking to her. The daughter gasps when her mother gives her the unusual name of someone she had been speaking to that very day.

During the break a gentleman who refers to himself as a rough diamond appears in my mind's eye. I share this with my friends. Kerry-Lee, who is also there to support me and a great medium as well, proclaims, 'Oooh go with it, I just love a rough diamond.'

Back in the room I discuss this rough diamond with the audience. My throat starts to feel as if it is being strangled. As a medium it is easy to misinterpret evidence; I could have said this indicates suicide by hanging but I feel this is not the case. I describe the feeling around my throat. A woman in the audience takes the message straightaway, certain this is her boyfriend, who passed many years ago after being strangled when his clothing was accidentally caught in a machine at work. His spirit is very humorous and passes information that is both relevant to his past and to what is occurring in her life right now. The love is obviously still there.

When demonstrating mediumship it is very important to bring through concrete evidence for the audience, the recipient and for the spirit world, to prove there is indeed life after life. Sometimes mediums bring through a typical grandmother with curly grey hair wearing an apron and holding a rolling pin. Even though this evidence is real, it is harder to prove as many people can relate to such a description of a grandmother.

The show goes so well, I am asked to hold a second demonstration a few days later. Early on I hear a spirit introducing herself to me as 'Nancy', saying she wants to speak to her granddaughter in the audience. The fragrance she wears is overpowering. I see bright red lips and what looks like an image of the actress Joanna Lumley from *Absolutely Fabulous*. Her hair is platinum blonde, pulled up in an extraordinary bun on the top of her head. She holds a cigarette in one hand and a drink in the other, and wears a short skirt and high boots.

This gorgeous grandmother points her bright red fingernails to the centre of the room, so I know approximately where her granddaughter is located. Her granddaughter looks a bit sheepish at first, but soon relaxes when she hears her grandmother's humour and the strength of her love. The audience is enjoying this delightful lady, who has everyone in fits of laughter, which is her way of showing love and affection.

Nancy tells her granddaughter that she will be joining in on her trip to the United Kingdom, is excited about her new ventures and that she has her darling poodle Jessie in spirit with her. The granddaughter's eyes fill with tears, especially when she describes the pink dog collar Jessie is wearing. Nancy's sister Irene had also recently joined Nancy in heaven; her granddaughter gasps in disbelief as she confirms the information. Details like this have so much meaning to the people receiving the messages, as they offer proof that their loved one lives on and is often with them.

My friend Mary comments afterwards: 'Kerry-Marie, you're a comedian as well as a medium. I enjoy watching you work as I can see the real character and personality of the person coming through, as if you become them. I can feel the love coming from their spirit is so real.'

It is touching to hear this. Even though connecting with loved ones can bring up unresolved grief, the humour and intelligence that also comes through from the spirit world is wonderful. When I finish a live demonstration, more information is often confirmed after the show and I become even more amazed at the power, intelligence and reality of the spirit world.

The next day after the show I receive a phone call from a lady who had been there the night before and had received a message from her grandson. She wants to let me know what a lovely surprise it had been and how it has comforted her greatly. Interestingly, when I described her grandson, I thought he had passed at the age of 17, but he actually died aged 22.

The healing began for her after the show as she realised he was 17 the last time she had seen him. He had spent most of his teenage life living with her, and they formed a very close bond over those years. Situations changed and his family decided to remove him from his grandmother, and she was not allowed to see him again. Five years later he decided to take his own life and did not have a chance to say goodbye to his darling much-loved grandmother. After the show she realised he had been showing himself at the age of 17, as this is how she last remembered him. She could not thank me enough because at long last she had the chance to connect with her grandson. After all these years she could now find some peace in her heart.

A few days after my first show I board a plane heading to the UK to sit my first practical exams under the Spiritualist National Union. Words said to me five years ago by a tutor ring in my head: 'You have been a beautiful butterfly your whole life and have been pinned down. The pin has been taken out and now you have been set free to fly and live the life you have been brought here for.'

I realise that I have now broken free.

## The journey begins

So here we are, where my journey begins. Born in 1961 in Auckland, New Zealand, I'm the fifth child in a family of six children. I'm the only daughter, and I was a real Daddy's girl. I adored my father. I have always loved to explore, have fun and spend time with people. I always tried to express myself in the most joyous way possible — little did I know the mountains that I would need to climb to get there.

Mum was a typical '50s wife and mother. It was expected that she would stay at home and take care of the family and think little of herself and her needs. From what I have been told she was a vivacious young lady in her youth who liked to have fun, and I think she would have felt tied down with the expectations of a large family and being there for everyone except herself. Finances were tight in the early days of my parents' marriage, further restricting my once vibrant mother.

Apparently when Mum arrived home with me from the hospital, all my brothers except one exclaimed 'Oh no, a girl! What are we going to do with a girl?' My dear brother Steven, now deceased, was apparently the only one excited to have a wee baby sister. He used to read *Goldilocks and the Three Bears* to me when I was very young; I can still see him there reading to me at night time. Steven was a sweet, warm and loving brother who emanated peace and love everywhere he went and lit up the world with his gorgeous smile. He proved to be a real child of God and later on an amazing brother, father and husband.

My first memory of the urge to break free occurred when I was a very young child. I can remember the great excitement when my father arrived home with a very large, shiny new Ford V8 car. It was an atmosphere filled with intense joy, happiness and elation. My brothers were scrambling all over this new vehicle, but my strongest memory is not being allowed to touch and feel the texture of this glorious addition to our family. Quite literally I wanted to break free from whoever was holding me back. Of course I was very young and did not understand the potential danger of climbing all over a vehicle without guidance and restraint; however my recollection is of feeling annoyed, and limited in what I was allowed to do.

Being an only girl with five brothers had a big effect on my childhood. I always longed for a sister. My mother told a story of wheeling me along in a pushchair; I was bawling my eyes out but suddenly stopped crying when I gazed upon two young boys having a fist fight. Mum said most little girls would get frightened if they saw such a thing but to me with four elder brothers it was normal and made me feel at home.

When my younger brother Matthew was born I was shipped off to my aunt's for a week. I can still recall feeling homesick and wanting to be with my own family. To this day I can remember being held upside down, while my hair was washed and my scalp scrubbed by my aunt, who was of course doing her best and probably feeling totally out of sorts. I was taken along to another aunt's house for a visit and overindulged in her yummy colourful sweets, which made me horribly sick at the time.

Christmas arrived not long after Matthew's birth. I was so excited to have a new wee baby brother for a companion. About that time, I can still remember the incredible feeling of waking up and discovering next to my bed a beautiful crib with a baby doll inside it. Receiving such a thoughtful, unexpected gift was amazing. It felt like a true gift of love from my family.

I adored my father from a very young age and used to eagerly wait at the top of our driveway for him to come home for lunch. He often said to me: 'Kerry-Marie, for I love thee.' He was a very special man and he will always remain dear to my heart. I can hardly remember any cross words between us and I felt totally loved by him. Yes, I was the 'apple of my father's eye', and in my eyes he could do no wrong.

Our house at the time had a basement area, which was later converted into a lounge. When I was about seven, Matthew and I decided the basement would make an ideal swimming pool, so we blocked up the door with Mum's towels and put the hose into the basement. It soon turned into a complete disaster, as we flooded the house and were promptly sent off to our bedroom in disgrace.

As a young girl I totally adored animals. I had a huge fascination for them all. In particular I was drawn to dogs; my father was aghast when he turned around to see his little girl with her arms wrapped around a huge German Shepherd. Our neighbour had a gorgeous boxer called Sheba who I would visit regularly; I would often sneak over just to play with their dog. I can still remember playing tug-of-war with Sheba with a long piece of flax when she got so excited she bit me. I was devastated that this darling dog would do such a thing.

As a little girl I totally embraced all 'girly' things; I loved to dress up as a princess or a ballerina. I would perform for visitors, who would often ask my mother 'Is your little girl a ballerina?' At one point I begged my mother to send me to ballet lessons, but she refused, stating it would be too much work to organise the costumes. Just before I started school I remember trying to persuade her to let me go to kindergarten so I could learn to play with other children but she said it was too difficult for her and I was not allowed to go. For some reason my mother was trying to protect me from the world that I just wanted to explore. I felt bewildered. Why could I not do all the things that other children were allowed to do?

I loved my brothers and always wanted to impress them — however I was known to say to my Uncle Jeff, 'One of me has a lot to put up with.' I must have heard that somewhere! I recall as a pre-schooler being delighted to find a piano in a room at a family function, and could not wait to entertain others with my own made-up tunes. The boys in the room put their fingers in their ears as I bashed away at the keys thinking I was totally marvellous.

My mother often used to walk to the local pharmacy down the road; I loved going into the pharmacy and marvelling at all the colourful glossy lipsticks and the shiny nail polishes. I couldn't wait to grow up and wear all this wonderful makeup myself one day. We would return home and she would make me hot cocoa and say, 'Now all the kids have gone to school, let's have a cup of cocoa and some peace.'

I loved being around people, getting out and about and exploring new and exciting things. Apparently, as a baby when my mother would take me out for the day, I was full of joy as I greeted all the people I met with a smile. I loved new experiences. When we returned home after a day's outing I would cry at the top of the driveway because I didn't want to go home.

I found it difficult later on as an older child, when my mother would say to me, 'You always want to be entertained.' It made me feel like there was something wrong with me. I was interested when my eldest brother, Bradon, told me that Mum used to say that to him as well when he was a child, and how much that affected him. It made me realise it was not just said to me and I was indeed just a normal child wanting to explore, learn and have fun.

Growing up I longed for Mum to join in and have fun with me, but she never seemed to be around very much. Looking back I wonder if she may have been depressed. She wasn't a practical person, and she did struggle with six children. As a young child I could only see things through a child's eyes and was not able to grasp what my mother must have been going through at the time.

Dad was always working in his construction business and was not at home a lot, and I feel in some ways my mother's life didn't turn out as she hoped. When I was young, I thought she didn't embrace her feminine side, but looking back at photos of her as a young woman she appeared very full of life, young and feminine. Somewhere along the line she must have changed.

I have a very strong memory of my mother's outstretched arms in the water with other ladies in the water at the Birkenhead wharf. She swam with me just that once; it was the last time she ever swam. I just wanted Mum to be happy but it seemed to be something she found hard to do; it was like she was preoccupied. I often heard her say, 'I brought my first four children up and I dragged up the last two.' Mum had a miscarriage before I was born and that may have been something she never got over properly. I know she often complained that my dad was never there to help her through the early years. I feel Mum must have felt lonely and lacked support with such a large family to bring up mainly by herself. She must have felt lost a lot of the time.

I can vaguely recall my grandparents; sadly they all passed away before I turned five. I have memories of Mum's mother, who I called 'Ma Ma', as being soft and gentle. She would always give me a piece of paper and pencil, and would whisper to me, 'I will give you a piece of paper and pencil in heaven.' Perhaps she knew that she did not have long to live. The visits to Ma Ma were happy and warm, and she seemed a very comfortable and peaceful person. In complete contrast to Ma Ma, I was terrified of my father's mother, who I knew as Grandma. I only have memories of her telling me off. Later in life, my mother told me that she had been quite a difficult mother-in-law. She said that at Grandma's funeral she heard totally different stories about her; her family saw her as a happy and vivacious woman. People's perceptions of their life experiences and how they see other people and situations can vary a lot from other's points of view.

My father's father, Grandad, was a soft and gentle man to whom I sang Christmas songs when I was five. I can still remember sitting on his knee and singing to this blind man 'Oh Christmas Tree, Oh Christmas Tree'. I thought I was pretty clever being able to recite these songs and could see that my Grandad was very proud of me. My mother's father had passed before I was born.

My brothers used to think it was fun to tease me, as you might expect being the only girl. When I was very young they would say to me, 'You are awfully nice.' I used to end up in floods of tears at the word 'awfully' as I didn't understand what they were saying. As funny as it seems now, the teasing did get a lot worse, and it was difficult for a young girl to deal with.

I wanted to spend as much time with my father as I could. Every Sunday my mother would dress me up in my Sunday best, hat and all, and our family would head off to church. At church I always wanted to sit next to my father. It became a ritual for him to give me the donation envelope to put in the plate as it was handed around. Then one dreadful day my father didn't pass me the envelope; it felt like a terrible rejection. It was clear even at a very early age that I had a sensitive nature.

As a little girl I started to sense energy and spirits around me every night. I was terrified of what I was experiencing. Every night I would wake up and crawl into my parents' bed so I could be next to my father as I always felt safe knowing he was there. I was often very frightened because of the energy I could feel. I could see people standing at the end of my bed, which I found terrifying. My parents decided to call these people 'the boogie man'. I often heard them say 'Kerry is seeing the boogie man again.' They told me over and over again this was just my overactive imagination and I was just afraid of the dark. My parents insisted that there were no such things as ghosts and they were just make-believe.

These experiences of sensing, seeing and hearing spirits, along with a lack of sleep, went on for many years to come. Every night was the same: the frequent visitors surrounded me, waking me up in a state of terror. I dreaded going to bed at night because I never knew what to expect. It was a lonely and frightening time, and I didn't know what to do.

# *Being the best child I could be*

Never Be the Same

Little girl you seem so haunted
Keeping everything inside
How often have I seen you
With such pain beneath your smile?
Is there a reason for your sadness
A method in your madness, logic to your style?
But there's a light shining on you
And there's a fire in your eyes
Yes there's a light shining on you
And there's a fire in your eyes
Father, how could you?
Brother, what's your game?
Uncle that we trusted
Things will never be the same
Things will never be the same
Things will never be the same
And now you're a woman
With a life and a family of your own

Don't you wonder how you made it?
Through the torment, the sickness and the pain
It took you thirty years to get there
And a billion others like you are trying to do the
same

And there's a light shining on them
And there's a fire in their eyes
Yes there's a light shining on them
And there's a fire in their eyes

Father don't you do it!
Brother, it's your shame
Uncle, friend, and stranger
Things must never be the same
Things must never be the same
Things must never be the same

© Bos O'Sullivan, 2008

There I was, at five years of age standing in a line of children, waiting to go into a school classroom for the first time. I can still remember the smell of freshly cut grass, the atmosphere of anticipation and the buzzing noise of children and parents talking. I was confused to see children around me crying and holding onto their mother's skirts — I was so excited about going to school. I just couldn't wait.

My first teacher at St Mary's School in Northcote was Sister Anne, and I just adored her. She dressed in a stiff white habit as she was from the Dominican Order; she was kind, happy and playful. My first year at school was mostly happy and full of fun. I loved it when I was asked to 'do the news', which involved standing in a cardboard box which doubled as a TV cabinet to present the news for the day. I remember being so upset when I came down with chicken pox and could not attend school. It was the longest few weeks in my life, recovering and just waiting to go back to my class.

In my first year at school my parents discovered that I was a very fast runner. I would sprint well ahead of the other children in my year, but would stop just before the finish line and not run through it, letting all the other children run past me. Mum was a fairly competitive woman when it came to sports and was determined to see me win so she told my brothers to stand on the other side of the ribbon to encourage me to run through. This worked a treat and in the following year to everyone's delight I won all my running races.

I'll never forget my very first school trip, to Little Shoal Bay in between Northcote and Birkenhead. It was summer time and I was in my second year of school. We went to the beach and were allowed to climb over rocks to see what we could discover, and much to my delight I found a tiny pink crab that I fell head over heels in love with. I just had to take this wee crab home to be my pet. Somehow I managed to get it back to school, determined to get this dear little creature home with me.

I was totally terrified of my teacher that year. Mother Margaret had fierce eyes and would stare at me and make me terribly nervous. For some reason she kept us back late that day and I missed my school bus home. I decided this was not a problem as I would simply walk home with my crab. I was three-quarters of the way up Onewa Road, when I looked up and saw my mother in her green Model-A car searching for me. She was not happy. I was severely told off and taken down to Birkenhead Wharf to return the crab to the water. I was totally heartbroken. Not only that, my mother was also furious with Mother Margaret for allowing a six-year-old to walk home by herself and so she wrote her a note that I was to take to school with me. I was too frightened to give the note to Mother Margaret so just hid it in my schoolbag. Some days later, the note fell out of my bag, and a goody-good girl called Veronica could not wait to pass the note on to the nun.

Mother Margaret called the class together and announced how this wicked child had told lies to their mother about missing the bus and how this girl would be condemned to hell where she would burn forever. I had terrifying visions of devil horns with burning fire all around me. Then Mother Margaret decided to punish me further and told all the children in the class to say in turn why I was such a bad person. Of course Veronica was the first to raise her hand, busting with judgemental observations that she blurted out in front of the whole class. I hung my head in shame, feeling really anxious and scared, not to mention terrified I would burn forever in hell.

Later that day, Mother Margaret got the class to stand to attention, her harsh, glaring eyes staring directly at me like they were piercing through me. I was busting to go to the toilet but I was totally petrified and wet my pants. Before I knew it I was standing in an enormous puddle. This infuriated her further and my brother Paul was called to help clean up the mess and get me onto the bus to go home, uncomfortable and ashamed. Thank goodness Paul came to my rescue.

Paul was very kind during those early years of schooling. He used to organise me and get me ready for school. I felt loved and taken care of by him. Then things changed. He was so kind, gentle and warm and then it all became different. I never knew what happened to Paul or why he suddenly changed, but for some reason out of the blue he became very distant and pulled back from me. The old Paul seemed to melt away, but I have loving memories of the kind brother that I know must still be in him somewhere.

Our school decided to put on a talent show for parents to watch and I was picked to participate. I accepted the challenge with great excitement. My only problem was that I didn't know which song to sing, so I asked Mum for some guidance. She was busy with visitors so she suggested 'Rock my soul in the bosom of Abraham', as she said it would be easy to teach me and I would be able to remember the lyrics. So there I am, this little six-year-old singing away at the top of my lungs 'Rock my soul in the bosom of Abraham', holding my arms in front as if rocking a baby. Everyone, including my mum, burst out laughing and I was so mortified. It was even worse when Mum repeatedly told this story in later years. I think parents can sometimes humiliate children without realising. It is so important to be mindful of children's sensitivity.

Meanwhile, my mother must have felt a little guilty about making me take the crab back to Birkenhead Wharf, because to my surprise one day when I arrived home from school she had bought me a turtle. I was completely over the moon and couldn't wait to come home each day to see my dear wee turtle, which I named Rhubarb. He was a total joy to me, my first real pet. I fell head over heels in love with the marvellous little creature swimming around his yellow pool.

Sadly I also have memories of rushing home to see my darling wee Rhubarb, and finding him on his back with his legs in the air. This was my earliest experience of death and losing someone or something I truly loved.

I was always excited to let my creative juices flow. At school we were taught how to make pompoms out of wool woven around a cardboard circle. I thought the whole thing was marvellous. My mother was quite a good knitter and had skeins of amazing soft wool, shiny gold knitting needles and half-finished pieces of knitting in her cupboard. It was so enthralling; I just wanted to learn to knit. Somehow I talked my mother into buying me some large, plastic size-one needles so I could make a start. I copied the other girls at school to try to work out what to do but needed some guidance from my mother, so I plucked up the courage to ask her. I can still remember my mother standing over me, exasperated as I dropped stitches. My hands were shaking first in excitement and then in fear from her reaction. I was desperately trying to understand this knitting business but my mother's dwindling patience, lack of tolerance and little time to give, made us both exasperated.

Looking back I can see that she simply had too much to deal with but I didn't understand her limits back then. I was a child full of love and happy energy and I just wanted to learn to express myself creatively. It was like she had no idea how my heart ached to be able to knit and create beautiful things.

Even now I remember my mother getting very cross with me and telling me that she didn't think I would be very good at knitting. I felt totally hopeless. That was virtually the end of my knitting days, even though I struggled to teach myself for a few years after that.

At the time it was very hard to understand why Mum didn't encourage me. As an adult now, I would say it was not because she didn't want to, but rather because she was so strung out, stressed and tired with a large family that were mainly boys. I would say she felt overwhelmed most of the time and simply did not have the energy to give to me. My father was working a lot and doing his best but I feel Mum lost a sense of who she was amongst all the chaos. Around that time my older brothers also seemed to enjoy teasing me a great deal to get a reaction. For a sensitive little girl it was not much fun and I slowly started to lose my confidence.

My mother told me in later years that when she was first married she was a good housewife and didn't mind cooking, but by the time I came along she really did not enjoy food preparation. I was sent to school with nearly stale, tasteless, brown bread Vegemite sandwiches that tended to be dry because they had been wrapped in lunch paper and frozen weeks before, to save my mother some time. One day Mother Margaret spotted me throwing my sandwiches away and she made me take them out of the rubbish bin. She decided to make a spectacle of me, making me eat these horrible sandwiches in front of everyone.

At the end of my second year at primary school, our class was selected to perform a Christmas play for our parents. Secretly I wanted to be chosen as Mary, but in the end I had to accept being an angel. I was so excited to be able to dress so prettily, and I couldn't wait to go home to tell my mother. My mother seemed very tired and not very enthusiastic about the whole idea so she found an old sheet in the cupboard, cut a hole in it, put it over my head and sent me off to school to be an angel. It was such a humiliating moment — there I was standing in a discoloured old sheet and as I looked around me, there were my school friends who were dressed up as angels in all their glory with beautiful dresses made out of chiffon, lace and sparkles. Some of them were even wearing tutus. I adored these beautiful dresses and of course Veronica was wearing the most glorious gown. Mother Margaret shuffled me to the back so I couldn't really be seen. Mum proudly attended this Christmas play and to this day I have to wonder what on earth she was thinking. Maybe she wasn't aware at the time. All I know is that I was so ashamed and embarrassed, but I never gave up hope that one day things might improve for the better.

Not long after Christmas my darling grandfather on my father's side passed away and I remember then that the terrible thought of dying and death really hit me. I came to the huge realisation that life on earth does not go on for ever. This saddened and worried me at the time, knowing that each day that passed by was a day gone in my life on earth. Little did I know what was in store for me in my future.

Thankfully, I moved on from Mother Margaret's class and at age seven I found myself in Mrs Johnson's class. She was an older English lady who was very well spoken with a very kind demeanour. I was particularly struck by her beautiful apricot nail polish. Around this time I became more aware of my love of movement, through both sports and dance. Any time we had a chance to practise dance at school I was elated and could not get enough of it.

My parents had bought me a Cindy doll as they were quite the thing back then and a little pink hand-sewing machine. I could not wait to get started finding old pieces of material and buttons around the house. I made dresses for my Cindy doll, hand bags and boots. Her first outfit was green with red stitching. The fact that I created these clothes myself made Mum and Dad very proud, and they decided I took after Ma Ma, who was an amazing sewer.

Mum began to really enjoy the horse races, and often on the weekend she would go to the local TAB to place her bets. It gave her a sense of excitement and I guess with my father always at work, this ended up being her main source of entertainment. Somehow betting on the races gave her comfort and solace of some kind.

Unfortunately it meant I was left at home unsupervised for long periods. One horrible day around this time, the sexual abuse started. It went on for five years. I had no idea what was happening. It was so shaming, awful and frightening and I felt completely powerless. I had no choice. I was an innocent seven-year-old with no understanding of sexual matters; I just knew about modesty and not showing certain parts of the body. Any discussion relating to sexual matters was very hush hush and taboo in our family.

Every time the abuse occurred I was threatened by the abuser that something awful would happen to me if I told anyone. To this day I cannot recall what the threat actually was and I still remain clouded about this. Something I do recall was being given money to buy sweets to keep me quiet. I was trapped and terrified and it was totally about someone else having complete power over who I was and my body. My boundaries were broken along with my spirit and even though the wounds of these times have been somewhat healed, I still have some deep scars. I will never be the same but I am stronger now through the power of healing and forgiveness.

Where were my parents when this occurred? My answer is that paedophiles are very clever people who know when to prey on their victim and how to control them. I am often asked 'Why didn't you tell your parents?' I was threatened and bribed not to tell anyone and also as a child I did not feel confident enough to tell them. I didn't know how to tell them, I was scared of getting in trouble and being told off and so I held the pain within for many years. I was manipulated into keeping some very unhealthy secrets.

I also have to admit that even though my mother did her best, I was scared of her and didn't know how to approach her about this subject. It was like she was a prickly porcupine. There was so much deceit. I turned the shame, blame and guilt inwards towards myself.

At that time of the abuse, I was being prepared for two sacraments of the Catholic Church, confession and Holy Communion. We were taught at our Catholic school that if we sinned we would go to hell. I felt so yucky, awful and powerless and somehow convinced myself that I was a bad girl for being abused. Perhaps I could tell the priest about it and then maybe I would be OK and would avoid hell and damnation. One day I plucked up the courage to tell the priest in confession that I had been rude, but when he asked me what I meant by that I was so ashamed I just said 'I was rude to a friend's father'.

I decided it was best not to talk about it and held it inside myself for many years. There was nobody I felt I could tell as it was confusing and dark. I felt trapped, with no way of getting out of where I was, and the biggest feeling I had was that there was no choice.

During the years the abuse occurred, I went into a sort of trance and stopped engaging with the world. My schoolwork started to suffer. When I came home from school my mum wasn't there. I had homework to do but never did it and nobody seemed to supervise this. My mother left a key out for us to let ourselves into the house after school and eventually she would turn up at home to cook what I considered a yucky dinner of fatty chops, cold lumpy mashed potatoes and cold cabbage. It was like my mum was going through the motions of life herself without really engaging in anything.

Between the ages of seven and 12 I did my best to embrace life. I continued to have a love for people, enjoyed plays and acting, loved to run and play sport, enjoyed my friends, nature, animals and life in general but inside I felt squashed, ignored and abused. The sexual abuse became interwoven into the rest of my life. I had to keep it to myself and learn to live with it. Slowly my self-esteem and confidence started to erode even further.

My first Holy Communion arrived. I was dressed in a white dress with frills around the neck and shipped off to my cousins', who put curlers in my hair. I ended up looking like a smaller version of my mother — I thought I looked hideous but my mother thought I looked glorious and was very proud of her creation. I went through it all with a smile on my face.

# *Elizabeth appears*

I have realised over the years that children are survivors. If their parents are not there for them, children will find someone else to do the job.

This was certainly the case for me. In my adult years, I forgave my mother and she became my greatest strength and my rock. However during my school years Mum seemed to live in some kind of hazy fog, not engaging in life. She was often angry or upset; looking back I see she was not happy and felt quite alone and trapped. I don't think she was suited to having a large family and more than once I heard her curse the Catholic faith for this. She felt the Church did not fully understand the consequences of being a mother with so many mouths to feed and so little time.

Our home was often in turmoil and my childhood lacked structure and certainty. I became very close to our neighbours, the Scott family — sometimes I practically boarded there. I befriended the Scotts' daughter, Loren, and we had a lot of fun together. She had two younger brothers, Neville and Ian, who I did not have much to do with. Mrs Scott was a marvellous person and in a very short time became my second mum. I just adored her and she did so much for me.

Mrs Scott introduced me to so many things. I stopped feeling ignored, bored and alone and she made such an effort to be there for me. This vibrant, happy lady seemed to understand so much about me. She took an interest in watching my netball games, she taught me how to swim, make clothes for my dolls, bake, iron and much more. When she realised that I couldn't tell the time or tie my shoe laces aged eight, as nobody had shown me these basic skills, she taught me in a way that made me feel loved and secure.

I sometimes felt I was a nuisance to Mrs Scott with my regular visits but she always made me feel so welcome. I will feel eternally grateful for Mrs Scott being in my life.

I can remember quite clearly how one morning she started talking to me about psychic people and how some people have a special gift or a 'sixth sense'. I was very intrigued by this, so she explained how some people just know who is on the phone when the phone rings or they think of someone and suddenly bump into them. Mrs Scott was a believer in such things but it was not accepted in my family. I can remember my mother telling me repeatedly that fortune tellers (or psychic people) were evil and it was a sin to indulge in these types of activities. Mum said those people would be punished by God and I convinced myself it would be a terrifying thing to become involved with. She told me that mediums were particularly evil and never to see one of those people at the fairs with crystal balls, as bad things would happen to me.

Mrs Scott even taught me how to raise budgies, when she saw my interest in birds. At the time, I owned a budgie called Bluey. He ended up with a girlfriend in the same cage and lo and behold, not long after that little eggs were laid. Oh my goodness, this was so exciting! I really thought that baby budgerigars would break through these little eggs and sprout into life but sadly this never happened. So Mrs Scott thought it would be a grand idea for us to build a proper aviary and with the help of her husband, that is what she did. She filled the aviary with budgies and before long baby budgies started to hatch. Mrs Scott would let me hold these delicate birds and sometimes assist with their feeding. Then I would watch these little baby birds sprout little feathers and transform into beautiful adult budgies. This was indeed a special time in my life.

Even though these years were fun with Mrs Scott, at home I was constantly hounded and pulled apart from bullying and sexual abuse. This was something I kept buried inside myself, right into my adult life. I was tormented and told to 'keep quiet'.

One day as I was walking home from school, a beautiful young girl appeared beside me. She was so pretty with long, shiny, black hair. She had a light olive complexion and she gave me so much peace and love. I felt nothing could hurt me with this imaginary friend by my side. I didn't know who she was until a lot later in life when she told me her name was Elizabeth. People often noticed me speaking to her and thought that I was talking to myself, but I wasn't. I was having long and intense conversations with my friend, who seemed to understand everything about me and loved me regardless. She seemed to give me happy, peaceful energy, love and a huge sense of femininity. She had a freshness that kept me positive whenever she was around.

I believe that during this time, Elizabeth was one of my main guides. She may be my guardian angel who was sent to help me. I feel Elizabeth did her best to protect me and tried to keep me safe. She was there for me to talk to and love unconditionally.

I will forever be grateful to darling Mrs Scott, who I feel Elizabeth made sure was in my life at that time to give me some joy and comfort.

The other beautiful woman in my life at that time was a friend of my mother, who I called Aunty Jennifer. She was such a wonderful woman, full of joy, love and enthusiasm. She was gentle, feminine and was always dressed beautifully in the most colourful clothes and shoes. She always brought one of her dogs with her on her visits to our house. I loved her to bits. Whenever I knew she was coming to visit I waited with baited breath all day for her to arrive, until she finally appeared at our doorstep in an adorable dress and shoes, arms laden with gorgeous iced cakes and other delicious food for us all to eat.

At times I was allowed to go and visit Aunty Jennifer. I would never want to return home because it was such fun. I loved to play with her dogs, and Uncle Athol and Aunty Jennifer even taught me to ride a two-wheeled bike. I felt very loved and cared for at their house. My mother would get angry when I came home as I didn't want to fit back in. She would say 'Kerry has her nose in a knot again.'

I kept dreaming my way through school; I never really enjoyed it and was happy to focus on sports, dancing, drama or any other creative activities. I did feel rather inferior to other children as they had the most delicious lunches and I had stale brown bread sandwiches. One of my friends, Amy, used to share her lunch with me as I just could not stomach mine. A lot of children seemed to have really nice clothes and I hunted through my brother's drawers and would wear their shirts as a dress so I would feel better about myself. I longed to dress up just like Aunty Jennifer. As a youngster, apart from second-hand school uniforms, I mainly wore T-shirts and shorts. I longed to dress up and be feminine and pretty — my brother's shirts seemed similar to a dress so I would wear them around because anything was better than nothing.

I continued to beg my mother to let me learn ballet but she still refused. She did sign me up to piano lessons with Miss Anderson, who was very short with bandy legs and strange black shoes. I wasn't very good at practising or doing my theory homework but somehow she managed to push me through to Grade 8. I was an accomplished piano player at one point in my life but, through lack of practice, my piano-playing ability has left me in later years.

Mrs Scott somehow talked my mum into letting me join the local running club, Calliope. For many years I was a successful short-distance runner, winning many running races and representing the club at competitions. My mother enjoyed netball and she and Mrs Scott supported me in this too. I enjoyed playing netball and played in either a Centre or Wing Attack position. Mrs Scott also took her children to gymnastics and sometimes I was allowed to join in even though I wasn't a member of the club.

Mrs Scott was forever doing fun things with her family. I remember her building trolleys with us all — my brother Paul also built a trolley and thought it would be a great idea to tow me up the driveway then let me go backwards where I toppled over and badly grazed my elbow and knees. He was severely punished by my father and given a smacked backside when he returned home.

One awful day my mother and father went out for an evening and left me at home with my brothers. It was a night I will never forget. A fight broke out — I can remember one of my brothers banging the head of another one on the kitchen floor. I went to bed a shaking mess with Elizabeth comforting me until I fell asleep.

Sadly for my mother, after that I stopped her going out with my father and leaving me at home all the time. As soon as she made plans to go for the night I would come down with some sort of sickness so she couldn't leave. It must have been quite hard for Mum but for some reason I never felt comfortable telling her the real reason I was terrified to be left at home alone with my brothers at night.

When I was about eight years old, my mother finally figured

out how much I adored animals. She announced that I was going to be allowed a kitten but I wasn't able to have him as a very young animal and he had to be properly toilet trained first and so on. He was at my Aunty Pat's house until he was old enough to come to our place, and I was constantly at my mother to take me to see him. He was the most adorable ginger cat with a white bib and paws and I named him Goldie. Finally he came home and we became inseparable. He would only sit beside me, not on me, and I sensed he was worried he would hurt me. Goldie was such a loving cat and he lived for about seven years.

Meanwhile I started developing a huge passion for horses; I could not get enough of them. I read as many books as I could find about 'Jill and her pony'. At one point our family visited Rotorua, an area well known for its steaming hot pools, bubbling mud pools and geysers along with the smell of sulphur, which smelled more like rotten eggs. We went to visit the Buried Village and I begged my father for some pellets to feed all the animals. I was totally in my element.

There before me was one of the most magnificent animals I had ever seen — a beautiful grey donkey. I could not keep my eyes off it. I stayed there for hours in its company, just me and the donkey. Suddenly I heard my father shouting my name out in a panic, until he found me staring in wonderment at this animal. For me it was love at first sight and it took quite a bit of persuasion to coax me away from this newfound friend.

My friend Amy and I had a great joint passion for horses at the time, and I remember trips with her to Whangamata where we would ride our imaginary horses through the sand dunes on wild adventures.

Amy had a great idea that we should go to a horse ranch together and learn how to properly ride and care for horses. Somehow I talked my parents into letting me spend a week with

Amy at a ranch. Of course I was going to fall in love with a horse, but much to my father's horror it was the skinniest, oldest and sickest-looking horse on the ranch.

My father came to pick me up from my week of adventures and I whisked him away to see my newfound friend. As I pulled my father's hand anxiously along the path so he could see my beloved new soulmate, the horse, which was called Lad, took one look at my father and semi collapsed in exhaustion. My father was not amused that I wanted to buy this old skeleton of a horse, but to me it was the most beautiful creature in the world. I was politely persuaded to leave Lad there and to come home. Later on I heard my father telling people about how Kerry fell in love with this ridiculously underweight animal and how he admired my love of all living things.

# *These days stay with you forever*

The day before my eighth birthday, my parents decided to take the family on an outing to Rangitoto Island. We boarded the ferry full of excited anticipation. My brothers were impatient to climb to the top of the volcanic island as quickly as possible, so on arrival one of them put my younger brother Matthew on their shoulders and off they went. I desperately tried to keep up with them but they were just too fast. My mother and father were walking at snail's pace, so I was a bit unsure about what to do.

I decided to keep going by myself, and catch up with the boys at the summit. Near the top, the track became really confusing and I didn't know where to go. I was feeling quite lost, when I saw Elizabeth next to me, pointing to a man nearby who had a little boy with him. I ran over to him and he took me under his wing and led me along the track. We seemed to walk for miles, and ended up missing the summit, going across it, down the other side and around the whole island.

Exhausted after a whole day on my feet, I walked down a track and saw my father running towards me with a huge smile on his face. He picked me up and gave me the biggest cuddle ever, swinging me in the air. He had contacted the police and everyone had been searching for me. I was even allowed to have a yummy bottle of Fanta all to myself. I can still remember the sweet refreshing taste as it hydrated me and put some energy back into my little body.

My father was a very hard-working man and his business was doing well, so he decided he had reached the point in his life where he could afford a boat. One of his associates had an old yellow and white outboard boat that my father, along with his brothers, decided he could repair. They were all very enthusiastic about this new boat and decided to patch it up, repaint it and sort the outboard engine out. Once this was complete it was time for them to take it out on the water, so Dad and my older brothers headed off on the boat to Rangitoto for the day.

It was quite late into the evening when they finally returned. Mum had started to get very concerned. Dad walked in with a sad look on his face as the boat had completely conked out in the middle of the channel. The repairs hadn't held and the boat had started to sink. Thankfully my father had been sensible enough to bring life jackets along as well as oars. Somehow they managed to get to safety but I am not sure what happened to the boat.

However, my father had caught the boating bug and he went on to purchase another boat which gave us all many years of fun. We would often go out on the boat, fishing and swimming, and even staying the night. Matthew and I had bright yellow fishing rods that would bend frantically with the slightest bite from a fish, and I still love fishing to this day. One teary morning I had to wave my father goodbye as he travelled over to Great Barrier Island with my older brothers; Matthew and I were left at home while they went on their wonderful adventure.

On one trip I can clearly remember my father catching a yellowtail — as he was reeling the fish in a large kingfish jumped out of the water and consumed the yellowtail, and my father boarded a magnificent kingie as well! Dad's brothers got involved with boats and fishing too, and before long they were all racing around the harbour and Hauraki Gulf in their boats enjoying many fun times together. Dad always packed the yummiest of lunches including pink-icing buns — I can still remember the treat of eating these buns out on the water as they melted in my mouth.

One afternoon Matthew, who was about seven years old at the time, slipped off the boat into the water and Dad quickly jumped in to save him. When he surfaced with my brother all Matthew could say was 'There are no fishes down there?'

I continued to see Elizabeth around me throughout this time. I was so happy spending time with my father on his boat, spending time around Mrs Scott and her family, swimming, running and playing netball. Often my family would notice me talking to my imaginary friend and say 'There she is talking to herself again.' I would see Elizabeth walking down the road beside me and remember one day feeling totally embarrassed as Mrs Scott drove by and waved out to me while I was chatting away.

The abuse was still occurring during this time, and I tried to pretend it was not happening to me. My cat Goldie was a great comfort. I remember starting to have destructive thoughts about my body and decided I was ugly and that boys would never like me. It didn't help that I had crooked front teeth which were a bit discoloured from being pumped with antibiotics for ear infections growing up.

When I was 10 my mum decided it was time for me to learn how to colour her hair! Each time she would ask me how much grey hair there was and when I told her she would go into a panic. This went on for many years, to the point where I decided that grey hair must be some terrible thing. After she would wash her hair I would get a report about how well I had coloured her hair and told off when it was not quite right.

Unfortunately this insecurity I had around the aging process resurfaced in my thirties when my own wrinkles and grey hair began to appear. It took me a long time to accept that going grey and aging is a natural process that happens to everyone.

One of my friends was fascinated by the way Mum used to get her bowl out to mix up the paste for me to paint onto her hair, and she thought it was hilarious how my mother used to carry on. When we were about 12 she suggested we contaminate Mum's hair colour so we tipped curry powder, soya sauce, tomato sauce, herbs, Vegemite and all sorts of things into my mother's hair dye and mixed it all up. To be honest, it was a lot of fun. There we were painting my mother's hair, trying to muffle our giggles. We were positive that Mum's hair would turn out bright orange, but Mum exclaimed that the colour was 'the best it has ever been'.

Mum was also on a constant diet. She used to have puffy snacks in her secret cupboard — I enjoyed pinching them as they melted in my mouth. She was overweight and unhappy with her life, so I decided that being overweight was a dreadful thing and something that was never going to happen to me.

Elizabeth continued to support me. She told me I was pretty, that she loved me, the abuse would stop soon and I would be free again. She gave me so much comfort and love through these years, as she still does now when I need her. She turns up very unexpectedly, making me feel loved, uplifted and consoled until I feel OK about myself again.

One evening I woke to see the spirit of my cousin Jim at the end of my bed. He told me he had just died in a car accident, but he was going to heaven now. He said he would be OK, and to always love and look to the light. I woke my parents to tell them that Jim had died in a car accident and that he had come to my room to tell me, but they wouldn't believe me.

Sure enough, the next day there was a phone call from my poor aunty in a terrible state because her son Jim had just been killed in a tragic accident. My mother and father would not talk to me about what I had said the night before. I vaguely remember the funeral and my aunty and uncle being in a terrible state of grief. I remember feeling sad and sorry for them. I couldn't really understand why I had seen Jim standing in my room but Elizabeth told me not to worry about it and that I would understand one day.

Elizabeth also supported me when Vinnie, a boy at school, started bullying me on the school bus. He would get off at the same bus stop as me and throw stones and threaten to beat me up. I would see Elizabeth standing beside me giving me love and for some reason every time this occurred, Vinnie would back off. Elizabeth also told me to get off at a different bus stop and this would stop happening. I successfully avoided Vinnie from then on, and the bullying stopped. Elizabeth was most definitely my guardian and protector.

Another time I was walking home from school and a teenage boy approached me and asked to have sex. Elizabeth appeared next to me and yelled 'Run Kerry, run!', so I took off in a huge panic to safety. My spirit friend stayed right next to me all the way.

# One door closes and another one opens

The abuse finally came to a sudden end. I was so very relieved to be free.

One sunny Sunday morning I remember looking in my mirror at home, aged 12, and I knew the abuse had stopped and I would be free again. The abuser had a girlfriend so I would no longer be needed for his sexual pleasure. The relief was immense; but unfortunately deep down inside the damage had already been done.

I can remember the age of 12 quite well. At intermediate I had a fabulous teacher called Sister Catherine, who introduced us to the buzz word of the time: 'interaction'. We were allowed to do creative projects and sing a lot of awesome songs as she strummed and played her guitar. This nun was very different from any other nun I had met, so school became fun and exciting that year and I progressed well. I managed to convince my parents to buy me a guitar and with the help of Mrs Scott I figured out how to play it.

Many of my friends started to get into makeup around that age, so one weekend I gave it a go. Loren and I put on some of Mrs Scott's blue eyeshadow. We thought that we looked marvellous and I proudly went home to show my mother who completely hit the roof and dragged me to the bathroom with a flannel and soap and scrubbed it off my face with no mercy. I can still remember how painful the soap was in my eyes.

Like all girls of that age I had started to develop, but my mother refused to take me bra shopping. It was starting to get a wee bit embarrassing, especially during school sports. One day one of the girls really teased me about this in front of everyone in our class.

I went home with my head hung low and plucked up the courage to ask my mother for a bra, as the girls at school had been teasing me. At the same time one of my brothers walked into the room. My mother was embarrassed to talk about such things, so in front of my brother she asked 'What, for those little rosebuds?' I was mortified and have no idea to this day why she reacted in such a strange way to this very natural and simple request. It was like she could not deal with such things and it was just all too much for her. At this point I started to dislike myself and my body even more.

Once again I felt Elizabeth's energy coming in around me, telling me that everything would be OK. To this day I am positive that Elizabeth worked her wonderful magic with my mother because not long after this my mother took me to the Glenfield Mall where I was allowed to purchase my first bra.

Thankfully my confidence returned after this and I was elected Captain of the orange athletics team at St Mary's. I was very proud to have this position, I just loved it. After about six months one of my friends told me it was very uncool to be a captain and talked me into resigning, even though in my heart it was something I really wanted to do. Looking back I can see people have often influenced me in or out of situations that are not really right for me. Part of breaking free is being able to think independently for myself about what is right for me.

About this time my parents agreed to take me and some of

my brothers horse riding at a local horse ranch in Albany. I had previously visited this ranch and knew that there was a very difficult horse called Gary who was slow, stubborn and very hard to control. I asked the organisers not to give me Gary but for some reason they insisted this was the horse I would be riding for the day.

So up the trail we go and I eventually got Gary to go up the hill. My older brother George was showing off and galloping ahead, whipping his horse while my younger brother Matthew was lagging behind, making his way very carefully up the hill. George, who was ahead of me leading all the horses, told me I needed to hit Gary with my reins to get him going and show him who was boss. I took his advice, which in hindsight was not such a good idea.

Gary bolted and apparently I fell off and was dragged, as my foot was still in one of the stirrups. Matthew found me lying on the ground and thought I had died. He ran to my parents and said, 'Kerry is on the ground and I think she is dead!'

I cannot remember much except being held in Elizabeth's arms as she sang angelic music to me. I had a sense of being at peace and somewhere else. Then I woke with a terrible headache and a huge graze on the left side of my head. Someone walked me down the hill and took me to hospital. I recall Mrs Scott making such a fuss over me when I came home. She used to bring me delicious sandwiches and cakes, and she explained to me that I would have a dreadful headache for a number of days but that I would get better in time. I was left with a terrible bruise and graze on the left side of my forehead which took some time to heal.

During my high-school years I attended Carmel College. My mother made a huge fuss about me being in the top class where I was required to learn both Latin and French. We all feared our Latin teacher, the very thin and severe Sister Mary, who used to tell the girls we were all 'bold, brazen hussies'. Ironically I can still recall chanting '*amo, amas, amat*' and so on, which are words of love.

Carmel College was such a strict school at the time. We had to wear ties, hats and school blazers if we were in the public eye on the street or on the bus. Of course as soon as the bus left the school all the girls tore off their ties, took of their hats, undid their top buttons and shouted with joy. All that we were taught was how to rebel against a silly set of rules.

It was at about the age of 13 or 14 that my mother started to let me go out with my friends during the day and I was allowed to catch the bus to the city to see the movies. I had made some really good friends and we would go to the movies and enjoy buying chocolates, pies and filled rolls, and run Jaffas down the aisle. We used to go to the very cool Cook Street Markets, where you could buy incense and hippy-style clothes. I must have worn my mother down in some way because we all took to wearing bright green and blue eye shadow and platform shoes, thinking we were extremely up with the play.

I didn't care too much for school work and tried to avoid it at all costs, continuing to enjoy sports, playing my guitar and learning to sing and dance. I had a natural talent for playing the guitar and singing and used to write my own songs. One of my cousins used to encourage me to sing at family gatherings and I was told by many people that I had a good singing voice. I had a vision that maybe one day if I worked hard enough I could actually sing in a band.

One morning at school a so-called friend turned to me and said I had an awful singing voice. She made some awful moaning noise and said that was what I sounded like. I was so sensitive and sobbed and sobbed. Her words really hurt; it broke my heart and I never sung again and gave up playing the guitar. Looking back I can see how she was jealous and wanted to knock me down and put me in my place. Once again I was influenced by another instead of being true to myself.

About this time I started working for my father's business part time in the office and saved up enough money to purchase my first bikini. My mother found out about it and burnt it. She told me that the Bible says that 'Females that cause lust in men should have a noose put around their necks and be thrown in the depths of the sea.' I was never allowed to accept boys' phone calls. One young man turned up at our house and wanted to speak to me but my father refused. I was taken aside by my father and told he loved me so much that he would walk across a field of cut glass in bare feet to save my life and how could I do this to him? My father told me I was a very beautiful young lady and he worried about me greatly and that I was to keep away from all boys at all costs as they were up to no good. I was told that sex was evil and the work of the devil.

I felt so suppressed and controlled at this time and was not allowed to grow up like other girls. My parents would not let me go to school socials. I was just like any other teenager wanting to learn and grow into adult life and so I started to rebel.

My friend Maria used to take me away to Whangamata where we would get up to mischief, it was so much fun. I remember sneaking Bacardi out of my parents' cupboard and putting it in a drinking bottle to take to the beach. We mixed it with Coke and both gagged at the awful taste.

I had met a boy by this stage who I quite liked, and we agreed to meet at Whangamata. He decided to take me for a walk into the forest and tried to get slightly sexual with me and I completely freaked out. To me it was like sexual abuse all over again. It terrified me, to be honest, and I found the whole thing totally revolting. I ran away and told him to never come near me again.

Despite what happened at Whangamata, I still wanted to

socialise. I was still interested in the opposite sex, but it was made to feel like a sin, and added in was a cocktail of guilt from the abuse. All my friends were socialising and seeing boys and to keep up with them I pretended to have a boyfriend named David. I even resorted to writing pretend letters from him which had some sexual overtones. Mum had gone through my drawers and found these pretend letters and I was taken to my father's office in complete disgrace. My parents never let on if they knew the letters were fake; they told me this was the work of the devil and burnt the letters in front of me.

At this time my mum began to be heavily involved in the Catholic Charismatic movement. She said she had the gift of prophecy and speaking in tongues and I used to hear very strange words come out of her mouth, which really frightened me. She tried to convince my father to join her at these meetings, but he did not become interested until much later.

I can clearly remember asking my father if he believed in God, because he used to always fall asleep at Sunday mass. He said he did and told me a very interesting story about his widowed grandmother, who lived with her son (Dad's father) in Calcutta, India. They lived in a new unit which had been built on the site of a burned-down house where 'evil things' had happened. Neighbours warned them that 'lots of strange things happen in this house, so beware'.

My great-grandmother was apparently a strong-minded Presbyterian lady, although she was happy to bring up my grandfather as a Catholic. At night time apparently there were a lot of physical phenomena in the house, with chairs moving, cutlery rattling and so on. My family believed this to be evil phenomena because one day at lunch a photo of my great-grandfather under a cross on the wall fell and smashed in front of my great-grandmother. She was aghast and took it as a sign, so went to the priest, became a Catholic and attended daily mass. Apparently the phenomena stopped. This story was yet another confirmation in my mind that being a Catholic was the only way to live your life otherwise bad things would happen to you.

# *The darkness starts to close in*

Dad decided to save the world by inventing an engine that could run on water, thereby solving the power crisis. We were out on the boat one sunny day when we heard about his plans. As we were sitting there munching away on our sandwiches my father started sharing with us his thoughts about energy and power. He said that power and water were the world's most important resources and that he wanted to build an engine that produced both. Once home my father started on his new project and worked day and night on it.

Meanwhile my mother kept giving her prophecies and speaking in tongues, which sounded so strange to me. I honestly wanted nothing to do with it, apart from the time I accompanied her to prayer meetings at the Auckland Cathedral because of the good-looking boys from Rosmini College who used to go too. I dragged one of my girlfriends along so we could socialise afterwards. We would get dressed up in our cool jeans, tight tops and load on the makeup to impress the boys. It was a good laugh.

One day my mother received a prophecy for my father about his engine and how to make it work. My father was fascinated, even though he had a very scientific brain. It wasn't long until

Mum and Dad started working as a team; my mother would receive messages and my father would interpret them to mean something for his engine.

The family construction business had been going very well, but Dad was becoming less and less interested in it. Soon Uncle Trevor hopped on the bandwagon with prayer meetings, prophecies and speaking in tongues. The business began to suffer.

In my teenage years, all I wanted was a normal life, but here were my mother, her friend, my father and uncle sitting around our lounge speaking in tongues. It was so uncomfortable. My parents put years and years into the engine project and in the end nothing really came of it. I have always wondered, what it was all about and was what they were doing real? My father certainly seemed to believe so and I respected him for this.

Around this time my mother started to put huge pressure on me to do well at school. After all, my four elder brothers had done very well academically, and Paul was even Dux of Rosmini College. Despite the fact that Mum had ignored me throughout most of my schooling life, it was expected that now I would achieve.

It was a difficult time. My parents ignored me for most of the time, as they were engrossed in their strange work developing the engine. I was put under immense pressure to succeed at school, and was not allowed to socialise or do any fun things with my friends. I was still playing the piano, studying for Grade 8 in both my theory and practical exams. My only pleasure came from netball, running, my cat Goldie and time with Mrs Scott.

I can remember those years well. I used to wake up in the middle of the night in a cold sweat, with a lump in my throat and a huge knot in my stomach. I was terrified I might not succeed academically and felt I would let my whole family down by not achieving School Certificate. I can't remember Elizabeth being around me much at this time as maybe I was too fearful, scared and anxious to be aware of her.

Around this time my darling brother Steve met his wife-to-be, Priscilla. She seemed so gentle and I loved her right away. I met her at a Guy Fawkes night and remember handing her a sparkler so she could have fun drawing pretty pictures. She had long, blonde, wavy hair, a sweet smile and seemed to have a sense of peace and serenity about her. My brother had decided to follow my mother and join the Catholic Charismatic movement and that is where they both met. I remember walking past Steve's bedroom and noticing his gorgeous blue eyes gazing into space — I could tell my brother was falling in love. I knew he would marry Priscilla and they would be very happy together.

A fixation with weight and dieting started to emerge in my teenage years. One morning at school my friend Marianne shared with me that she had a real battle with her weight and did not know how she was going to get slimmer. Up until that time I never really worried about my weight — I just ate whatever I liked and thoroughly enjoyed my food. My father was very interested in nutrition, and I had an interest in biology and the human body, so I told Marianne I would write her a weight-loss diet to follow.

With dreadful timing, two events then happened which made me want to exert some control over my life. One of Mum's sisters, who was particularly weight-conscious, told me I was a little chubby and 'needed to be careful'. I started to feel self-conscious about my body.

My father's sister, Katrina, was divorced and in need of somewhere to live. She was a difficult person to be around because of her OCD; for example, she had a real thing about her seams and was always asking us to check if her seams were straight. My father tried to build her a flat under our house so she had somewhere to live. Every afternoon for three months she took me to the bathroom and got me to stand in front of the mirror and compare my thighs with hers. She told me that I was getting fat and that I really needed to do something about it. Unsurprisingly I started to get a huge complex about my body image. When I think about this time it truly does make me cry inside.

I decided it was time to fix my body and lose weight and studied quite a bit about diets, calories and what to eat and what to avoid. I started on my first diet and started to lose weight. My legs slimmed down and I felt much better about myself. I continued to have enough energy to play netball but I also continued to diet as it made me feel good about myself and it was something I could control. Unfortunately it became obsessive and I started avoiding situations where people would give me fattening food. I began to avoid Mrs Scott's invites to her house after school in case she would offer me food.

Around that time, my darling cat Goldie was run over. Dad came home from work especially to tell me. I was wracked with grief. I had no idea how I was going to cope without Goldie in my life. She had been such a comfort throughout such difficult years. I felt so alone, and grief-stricken to lose my wonderful pet.

My mother continued to put pressure on me. I had to be in the top netball team, to excel at school (I received extra maths tuition) and she also decided I needed to become outstanding at sewing. I had showed some talent and inclination at sewing when I was younger, and because Mum couldn't sew she was insistent that I attend private sewing lessons.

I suppose from the outside it would appear that my mother was supporting me with my schooling, but the truth was that she had ignored my schooling for years apart from that one year in primary school when I fell back. Every night my parents were having lunatic prayer meetings and I was just a nuisance, but at the same time I was being forced to perform at my music, schooling, sports and sewing.

The night sweats continued. I was so afraid that I would not pass my exams. My obsession with losing weight continued and my weight plummeted dangerously low. By the age of 16 I weighed 40 kilos. Yes, I passed my School Certificate in five subjects, to the great relief of my mother, but I was a very sick girl. I had lost interest in netball, running and swimming, I had no energy and I had isolated myself from my friends and the world in general. I would sit in front of the heater for hours as I felt so hopelessly cold. At first my mother didn't seem to notice my weight loss but after a time it became painfully obvious and I was shipped off to a variety of doctors, specialists and naturopaths to see if they could fix me.

Often anorexic females feel controlled by their mothers, and when I was trying to recover from my anorexia I certainly felt annoyed that my mother wanted to control everything. She was apparently given a prophecy from God about some strange diet I had to follow to get my health back again. I was made to eat terrible mushy concoctions that tasted disgusting and made me feel worse. I just wanted to be left alone. This eating disorder was not only an obsession, it was an escape and a dark, negative friend.

Steven and Priscilla decided to get married and I was invited to be Priscilla's bridesmaid. I jumped for joy at the prospect of it all. My mother worried that I was too thin and I would not be able to perform the task of a bridesmaid, and she insisted that I wear layers and layers of clothes so I didn't look too awful. It was just like my mother to worry herself sick about what people thought. The wedding went very well. Priscilla looked so pretty and Steven's blue eyes just shone with so much love for his darling wife.

Not long before the wedding Steven had a terrible accident where he dislocated his shoulder. While he was under the influence of morphine he apparently could not stop talking about me.

Over the Christmas holidays when I turned sweet 16 I travelled with my parents and Mathew to Great Barrier Island as my father and uncle had purchased some land there. My uncle and his family stayed on the boat and we were dropped off on the land to pitch a tent there. It was the most boring holiday of my life. We were totally isolated and there was nowhere to go apart from a stony beach. My father busied himself making steps up to the top of the hill. I got the feeling he was upset about my eating disorder and didn't know what else to do.

I made my mind up that summer that I was sick of anorexia. I wanted to be healthy again. Once we got home Elizabeth appeared to me; it was so nice to see her as she hadn't been around as much. She told me that I needed to tell my father of my troubles but I kept them a secret for a while longer.

Everyone wanted to have their say in how to best help me to overcome anorexia. A family at church whose daughter had a similar problem called a meeting with my parents. I don't know what was said but Mum and Dad were furious with me when they came home as they had been embarrassed.

I kept on pushing myself to eat normally and get back on track. I found that I had to take time eating my food, but I would get there. One afternoon I ate a beautiful chicken dinner and took my time eating it but Steven somehow thought it would be helpful for him to tell my parents that I hadn't eaten my dinner but had thrown it away. It was so unfair being ridiculed when it was so far from the truth. I had been trying so hard and just finished eating the whole dinner, but my parents believed my brother over me.

Then at school one of the nuns decided she would have her penny's worth too, and took me aside to sort me out. I had started eating normally again but I was still quite thin and stressing about doing well at school. The nun kept on sneaking up to me at meal times and spying to see if I was eating.

In the end it was simply all too much. I wanted to get away from this nun so I decided to leave school. I finally had a heart-to-heart with my father about my anorexia and admitted it properly to him for the first time; he was so loving and so caring and did not judge me at all. He understood I wanted to leave school and approached the bank manager to see if I could get a job at the local Bank of New Zealand in Birkenhead. The nuns at Carmel took my parents aside and tried to convince them to keep me at school because my marks were so high. I was determined to leave school to start my job, and it was a decision I never really regretted. To make up for not passing my University Entrance, I studied and passed UE English when I was 21 to prove that I could.

The interesting thing was when I slowly moved myself out of anorexia, even though it was a constant battle, my mother said that my personality changed. I feel it did as well in some ways as I used to be a free, loving person, but not as outgoing or talkative as I am now. After this sickness, I became more open and expressive. Maybe it was about getting some control back in my life and breaking free.

My anorexia started to leave me when I was 17. Falling in love helped this process to begin. Since then I have found that when an anorexic girl falls in love their eating disorder can very often leave them. I was transferred to the Northcote branch of the bank and a young man called Gerry used to come in every day with a school friend. Apparently he was very taken with me. Gerry eventually asked me out on a date to the hot pools but as I did not want him to see me in a bikini I said it had to be something like ice-skating or nothing at all.

My mother hit the roof and said I was not to go out with him and she felt he was so much older than me (he was 19 and single but had a moustache) and said he looked like an older married man that could have children or be divorced. Gerry however was quite determined to take me out on a date so he met my father and mother to ask their permission. We went ice skating together and he held my hand and my heart went into a flutter. Later on he was my partner for the Catholic debutante ball where I was presented to the Bishop. I was so happy to have Gerry by my side. I used to love to watch him play soccer at the local Takapuna soccer club and we would all socialise later. It was so much fun.

My psychic abilities started to develop while I was at the bank. I knew that one of the staff members, who seemed to be liked by everyone, was stealing money somehow. I used to see him go through office entries with a worried look on his face. One day my boss asked me to answer the phone as the receptionist was busy, and I turned around and said 'Is xxxxxx stealing money?' He looked at me with a shocked look on his face and asked me how I knew. I told him I just had a feeling and suggested he look at the office entries which were the key to how the fraud was happening. The thief was caught and jailed for a number of years, and from that time on my intuition seemed to get stronger and stronger.

One sad day Gerry ended our relationship. I was heartbroken, and a dark cloud came over my life at that point. I believe Gerry had been sent to me to bring me out of my anorexia and to show me love and happiness and that I was indeed a loveable girl.

Not long after my relationship with Gerry ended I unfortunately got involved with a new man, Phil. He seemed fun and exciting but the relationship left me in a grey and not so nice place. Gerry then decided he wanted me back but I felt it was too late to turn my back on Phil, who I felt was very controlling. I began to feel trapped again.

There is always a lesson to be found in the choices we make. By staying in a relationship that was not right for me, I began to understand the consequences of my actions. I was learning the lesson of cause and effect.

# *Into the light*

I knew in the long run that working in a bank was never going to be fulfilling enough for me. I really wanted to care for others, and decided to train to be a nurse. Instinctively I knew it was the right path for me to take.

I would often talk to my father about wanting to one day work in the nursing profession, but he never looked happy when I raised this. In his eyes, the job was too hard for his darling daughter. He wanted to keep me safe, and told me that working in an office was a much more suitable job for a young lady to pursue.

Gerry supported my interest in nursing, and had suggested I investigate training in general nursing like his sister. However after leaving Gerry my self-esteem started to drop significantly. I did not feel happy or empowered in my new relationship, instead feeling out of control and not good about myself. I did get on very well with Phil's mother however, and she became a lovely friend to me for about three years.

I struggled to have a normal intimate relationship with Phil, as I really did not enjoy it. I would clam up and just go along with it. To be honest it felt like the abuse all over again. Looking back, I can see I felt ugly, disgusting and quite depressed. I didn't take much care of my appearance and how I looked; I lost a lot of confidence.

Eventually I applied to be an Enrolled Nurse and was called in to meet the Matron for an interview. She questioned me intensely and gave me a very hard time about leaving school in the sixth form. I explained that I was immature at the time and it had been a silly thing to do, and that I had grown up since then. To my great surprise and delight I was accepted into the hospital system to train as an Enrolled Nurse.

I started off with great enthusiasm and loved living in the nursing home in Greenlane. I went from undereating to overeating; my weight was like a yoyo and I didn't feel good about myself at all. Happily, I loved my nursing studies and totally immersed myself in my work. At first I was working at National Woman's Hospital and was terrified to pick up these tiny little babies as they looked so fragile, darling little things. There I was, an 18-year-old girl showing mothers how to breastfeed. I enjoyed my time at National Woman's Hospital; I worked in the delivery suites and in intensive care where I would feed and look after premature babies. After a while the staff gained confidence in me and I was allowed to work with the very premature babies who needed extra-special care. I used to look up at times and see loving, caring spirits and angelic figures around the wee premature babies. The spirits emanated such love and care, their energy was amazing.

When I was transferred to Greenlane Hospital to work in the medical wards I was not very confident. It took a while for me to really get into the swing of looking after the medical and geriatric patients. I was transferred to the ear, nose and throat ward, working for a wonderful charge nurse named Sharon. She was so energetic and positive and I felt more able and confident when I worked with her. I felt Elizabeth around me a lot at this time. She repeatedly told me that I would not be staying with

Phil, as I was outgrowing him, but he had come into my life for a reason.

I went back to National Woman's Hospital and started working in the gynaecological wards, where I enjoyed the fast-moving pace of working in a ward where patients were admitted, had surgery and then were nursed back to recovery before leaving to get on with their lives. I found this work very satisfying and enjoyed the relationships that I formed with my patients.

I clearly remember one lady in this ward who had terminal cancer of the ovaries. I became very fond of her and I would stay two to three hours after my shift to take care of her as she was so frightened of death and she would not let me leave. I could see her life fading quickly and also just how frightened she was. The charge nurses could see how much I cared for her and didn't mind me staying late as they could see the lady really needed me. I still can remember when I came on duty one morning and she had passed away during the night. My nursing friend Moira and I were given the duty of laying her out.

Something interesting happened when we did this; as we rolled her over a gasp of air escaped from her lungs which can often happen after someone has passed, and, as upset as we were, we both got the giggles. It was like it was a way of releasing our nerves and emotions. I then looked up and saw her spirit staring back at me with her vivid blue eyes. She winked, smiled, then nodded her head and left. My friend was looking at me as she saw me staring across the bed. 'Anyone would think you've seen a ghost,' she said. I felt I could not share my story with her, so I kept it to myself. I really did not understand what was happening to me and I why I kept seeing things.

Throughout my nursing training there were various practical and theory tests to sit and I always seemed to do well. I was very nervous about the upcoming exams to gain my final qualifications as an Enrolled Nurse. Off to tech we all went, in Mt Albert, to sit the final exam. To be honest, I did not find the exam easy. When I came out, one of the girls in my class proclaimed to all that it was super easy and that she had passed the exam with flying colours. I felt dismayed but then saw Elizabeth in front of me smiling and winking, and I knew I would be OK. I had a strong sense that this girl was boasting and although she was very intelligent, she would not pass the exam. I was correct, and in fact I was one of the highest-achieving students. This gave me confidence to believe I could really do something. I could make it.

Not long after I completed my exams and qualified, I decided to leave National Women's to work at the Mercy Hospital, which was known as the Martyr at the time. When I first joined this Catholic private hospital, I wondered what on earth had hit me. These nuns were so strict and seemed to be very concerned about how tidy the patients' beds were, that the towels were hung the right way and silver service was a must. I have to say though, despite their pedantic ways, my standards of nursing certainly improved.

During this time I was still in my relationship with Phil, which did not seem to be getting any better, although my relationship with his mum went from strength to strength. I don't know how this happened but Phil and I ended up getting engaged, much to the horror of my parents, who were constantly telling me how much they disapproved of him and our relationship.

I still remember one night when we went out with friends; one of his friends said to me, 'I can't believe you are with him, you are beautiful, what you are doing with him?' That night I felt Elizabeth's presence next to me and she gave me this feeling of great strength, calmness and peace. I knew it was time to move on from my relationship with Phil. I was more worried about leaving his family and upsetting his mother of whom I was very fond. My own mother was very jealous of my relationship with Phil's mother.

I met Phil for lunch the next day and broke the news to him and of course he was devastated. As awful as it sounds, a weight had been lifted from me. I was happy and peaceful. Overnight I blossomed and became a totally different person. My mum had invited my totally gorgeous and funny Aunty Ada up to stay, and as soon as I walked into the kitchen she said, 'Kerry, you look like a girl that has fallen head over heels in love, not just broken off an engagement.' These days Aunty Ada's spirit often visits other mediums — she always makes them laugh. She was beautiful on the outside and on the inside as well.

At this time in my life I decided that I had to turn my life around. In my mind, Catholicism and my faith were the answer to everything. Interestingly, I still remember a vivid dream where I was flying over fires with evil groups of people bunching together in groups and I heard a voice say 'Your mother's prayers have saved you'.

I became a happy, fun-loving, blossoming 21-year-old with my whole life ahead of me. Being single did not worry me in the slightest. I dated lots of different men and had a lot of fun over that time while still hoping and waiting for Mr Right. I had decided that I was a 'no sex before marriage' type of girl and I have to say most of the young men that dated me respected this.

Meanwhile I started running quite a bit and sometimes I enjoyed doing this with Mrs Scott, my old next-door neighbour. She had shifted house but I still went to see her from time to time. Also, I took up tennis and enjoyed playing against my younger brother Matthew, who would get quite annoyed at me if I managed to beat him. I remember letting him out at the traffic lights one day to walk home as he was so miffed that his older sister had thrashed him at tennis. I enjoyed my pursuits with him and his friend Pete — we would go to the hot pools, where we used to have great fun together going on the crazy slides. I embraced the feeling of freedom at this time, the feeling of breaking free, being able to breathe and be myself again.

I can recall that after a while I started to feel a wee bit lonely and began craving a new relationship. Even though I was religious, my intuition was so strong. I could sense and feel things all the time, it certainly would not leave me alone. When I used to go down to the reception area to meet patients I knew instinctively how to make them comfortable. By the time I had taken them up to the ward and settled them in with a cup of tea I had totally won them over. I used to get up early and have breakfast with Dad before work; he loved hearing about my work and the dates I went on. He would always refer to me as his 'darling ray of sunshine'.

I was transferred to a very demanding surgical ward at Mercy Hospital, and was quite terrified of the Charge Nurse. I worked so hard to please her and the patients that it took a toll on my health, which took a bit of a dive. My well-meaning father was concerned and phoned the hospital about how hard I was working, and I was transferred to a less fast-paced geriatric ward.

Looking back this was a not a good move for me. I was not happy there, even though I enjoyed nursing the old people. I made friends on the ward and got on well with the charge nurse, but the staff tended to gossip a bit. Maybe they did not have enough to do; in my experience people who are not busy enough in their work or life like to create gossip or drama to add a bit more colour to their world.

I decided then that I was not happy working in a geriatric ward. I felt my career had taken a step backwards, so I applied to become a General Nurse which was not an easy thing to do. I applied at a number of hospitals to see if there would be any openings for me.

I was invited for an interview at Thames Hospital. The night I received this news, Elizabeth came to me and said 'It is not a good idea to go to Thames, you are better off staying in Auckland.' I had decided as a devout Catholic that I was not going to listen to this spirit friend and thought I knew better. On the way to Thames for the interview, a song came on the radio: 'Don't cross the river if you can't swim the tide'. It came on right as I was about to cross the Thames River. I went for the interview somehow knowing I was going to be accepted and that I was going to really regret my decision.

I did get accepted but kept fighting against my strong intuition not to shift to Thames. I went around everyone to get their opinion, encouragement and support and they all seemed to say 'go for it' but I just knew deep down inside it was completely the wrong thing for me to do. I kept hearing the song on the radio: 'Don't cross the river if you can't swim the tide'. Looking back it was my guides trying to suggest not to accept the position in Thames, but I refused to listen.

So off to Thames I went. When I arrived I was put into the nursing building with all the other girls, but something did not feel right. There was a lot to study and things became worse and worse for me. My fellow students were lovely but I felt so homesick and just didn't want to be there. It was academically challenging, the food was very stodgy and the hospital standards were completely different to what I was used to. One of the other nurses and I would travel home every weekend; neither of us really liked it there. The travelling back and forth, the lack of sleep and the anxious, depressed and lonely feelings took their toll.

My father was very encouraging and took a real interest in what I was doing so offered to help me. My sister-in-law, who was also a Registered Nurse, offered to give up her free time and assist me as well. I was very grateful for all their support and I ended up getting an A+ again. However I was so unhappy and miserable in Thames. I found it hard to go back to being a student nurse again, when I had previously been given so much responsibility as an Enrolled Nurse in the surgical wards. I felt so homesick, I didn't know if I could cope. I just wanted to leave and come home.

A really lovely couple in Thames invited me and a friend over for dinner one night. It felt so cosy, warm and happy that I decided the answer to all of this was to find a husband, get married and have a baby. I thought this would fix all my problems, so I made a definite decision to leave my nursing career and return to Auckland.

My parents were not happy about this turn of events when they drove to Thames to pick me up. I remember feeling exhausted, anxious and a complete wreck.

When I returned home, I completely collapsed on my bed in total exhaustion. I was lying on my bed trying to find some peace when Mum came rushing in and bellowed at me, 'Just because we brought you home, don't think you can lie around and do nothing with your life.' I felt even more of a mess.

A few days later I was on the hunt for a new job, and decided I was going to give nursing a wide berth for a while. I caught the bus into the city and started door-knocking in offices asking for a job. I quite clearly remember on one occasion a gentleman from one of the businesses in the city taking me aside and saying to me 'You are a remarkable young woman, not many people would be brave enough to go out knocking on doors and seeking work. You have an amazing future ahead of you and you have a great strength of character.' I can still remember his words.

Not long after that I managed to get a job as a private secretary at a company called Hick Brothers, at their head office in Parnell.

## *Finding me again*

Working as a personal secretary was a challenge to start with, as I had to sort out the company's filing system. My father made some helpful suggestions about how to do that. Once I had the filing in order I started to feel very bored as there wasn't enough to do. Saying that, I still felt terribly burnt out, so this job gave me time to recover from my ordeal in Thames.

Over time I seemed to get better and better, but I knew that being a personal secretary was not really for me. With the Christmas season looming, I decided that the company needed to decorate their offices (something that had never been done before at this company), so I took it upon myself to ask the Personal Secretary to the General Manager to ask for special permission on my behalf. She came beaming into my office to tell me the good news and it was like I had breathed some life back into the office again.

Towards the middle of the following year, I remember feeling cold and lonely, but also quite happy to be single at the time. My hands were always freezing. I used to say 'Oh well cold hands, warm heart,' and laugh it off.

One night I had a very vivid dream that I was at Auckland's

waterfront looking out to sea, feeling cold and lonely, and all of a sudden I felt a man's arms come around me from behind and embrace me. I can remember to this day the amazing feeling of peace, love and warmth from this dream.

The next day I accompanied my mum to the races, for something to do over the weekend. I remember feeling quite alone and depressed this particular day. I needed to go to the bathroom, and as I walked into the ladies area I was feeling terribly low. I looked up and there on the wall was a beautiful picture of a bride at the waterfront, in the same place exactly that I had seen in my dream the night before. I knew it was a sign that I would meet a husband and all would be well in my life. The photo gave me a sense of peace.

One of my family members kept suggesting that I needed to attend a Catholic weekend retreat called 'the choice weekend', where people about my age met together. I decided to take part, much to the disapproval of my mother, who seemed to worry about anything that was slightly different. I can remember a disagreement with my mother the night before I was supposed to go, so I decided I wasn't going to attend after all. For some reason she then changed her mind and pushed me into going.

When I arrived, I was put upstairs in a blue room that was very peaceful. A wonderful calm feeling came in around me. I had not seen Elizabeth for quite some time, but as I was lying in bed I had an amazing feeling of calmness and serenity come over me. Once again Elizabeth appeared in my room, transparent with a glistening glow around her. She had long black, shiny, wavy hair and the most glorious white dress. Whenever she appears to me she always looks like this and when other people have picked her up in meditation when I have been in the room with them, they always describe her exactly like this too.

Elizabeth had a message for me. She told me that this course was going to be life-changing. She said not to worry, and she would be back to speak with me again, that she was guiding and looking after me and to always remember that.

That evening everyone gathered together and we played games and shared stories. A nice young man called Thomas was sitting in front of me and as I felt quite rebellious at the time, I decided I was not interested in trying to impress him. For some reason I told him that I thought this whole weekend was stupid and I simply did not want to be there. He seemed to be fascinated with me and we ended up spending most of the weekend together. The main thing I learned from the weekend was that I was not the only confused mixed-up person in the world; there were others just like me. I realised other people had problems as well and in fact it was quite normal.

Thomas seemed a reserved sort of guy. I admired his calm energy, how he seemed to really enjoy eating his food and fitting in with everyone. I learned he came from a Dutch family and that he was really into deer-stalking, which I thought was a bit strange as I adored animals so much. When he was leaving in his blue Ford Cortina, he stopped to say goodbye and I cheekily bent down and kissed him on the lips. He seemed totally taken aback and I remember thinking, 'Oops, I did the wrong thing there.' We did not exchange phone numbers and I thought I would never see Thomas again.

About a month later I heard my mother talking on the phone, giving someone the third degree about why they wanted to speak with her daughter (I was 22 at the time!) She passed the phone to me and I was so embarrassed to hear Thomas's voice. He asked me out to the movies, I agreed, and he said he would come over to meet my parents and then take me out.

Thomas came to meet my parents as promised, and my father in particular was very impressed. When I woke up in the morning, Dad decided he needed to interrogate me about my date with Thomas. To be honest I was not sure about the whole thing and whether we were truly compatible, even though he seemed to be a nice young man. My father was convinced that Thomas was the man for me and that I should marry him as he was a decent young man, he was Catholic, he had a good job and he would look after me.

Throughout the years I had built up so much admiration for my father I decided that he must be right. Instead of following the natural process of getting to know someone over time I was convinced because Dad said so. Sure enough, Thomas proposed after we'd known each other for only one month. Six months later we were married at St Mary's Church in Northcote.

# The family begins

Fairly soon after we married I started to feel quite nauseous, and sure enough I was pregnant with our first child, Benjamin. It was all so quick! I met Thomas, a month later we were engaged, six months later we married and nine months after that we had our first child.

The birth was not an easy one and I ended up having an emergency caesarean section which really weakened me. Benjamin was a darling child but seemed to want to feed constantly and not sleep. I fell into the despair of being a first-time mother trying to care for a newborn baby while battling complete exhaustion.

As Benjamin developed from a baby to a toddler it became apparent that he was hyperactive (now called ADHD). I did a lot of research on the subject to try to understand my child's behaviour. Some people accused me of being a bad mother who did not know how to discipline my child, and this only led to more hurt and despair. One thing I feel did not help Benjamin was a course of antibiotics prescribed for an ear infection when he was nine months old. Benjamin developed terrible allergies, and even now as an adult he has problems taking antibiotics.

Throughout my life I have always had a huge love of Jesus

Christ and often wished that I could meet Jesus one day. One night around this time I did meet him, in a dream. I was in despair over Benjamin's behavioural problems, and my brother Steven, who was Ben's godfather, decided to come and pray over him one night. Steven told me he had received a message from the Holy Spirit that my son had ear problems.

That night I dreamed I was at home and Jesus phoned me and said he was coming over for a cup of tea. I told him he could not come now as my house was too much of a mess but he insisted and said, 'I am on my way, daughter of little faith.' Jesus arrived at the door wearing a long white garment with another maroon garment over the top. I immediately went down on my knees and begged for Jesus's forgiveness for any sins I had committed over the years. He said, 'Daughter, rise off your knees and take a seat over there. I am not interested in your sins, I am only interested in your faith.' At this time Benjamin came up in a very cheeky voice and said, 'Hello, Jesus.' I told Benjamin off and said, 'Don't speak to Jesus like that.'

Jesus laughed and put his hand on Benjamin's head and said, 'He is my child too. You think you love your child — you have no idea how much I love your son.' He then knelt before me and said, 'Kerry, do you know what faith is?' I told him it was about believing everything I had been taught about the Catholic faith, going to church and not sinning. He shook his head and said, 'Faith is doing things for others and not telling anyone else you have done them.' The love emanating from Jesus was incredible and to this day I have never felt anything quite like it. The Jesus I met in this dream was nothing like the Jesus I had been taught to believe in. He was loving, kind and not in the slightest bit judgmental. He was pure love.

I woke up from my sleep to see a magnificent white light over my bed and then I drifted off to sleep again. In the morning

Benjamin came bounding into our room, saying 'Mummy, guess what? Jesus was in our house last night.' I was speechless and told Thomas about my dream, and he believed what I had experienced was real. Then to top it all off Steven's wife (who is also Benjamin's godmother) turned up with a special plaque for us and it said 'Jesus, bless this house'.

After this incredible experience I was then led to visit a new GP, who sent me to another GP who specialised in allergies and used kinesiology. To our amazement, we confirmed that Benjamin was not only allergic to cocoa, colours and flavours but that he also had an intolerance to salicylate, which is a natural preservative in fruit and vegetables. He gave us a list of foods that were high in salicylate to avoid, and suggested we gave him food that was high in protein.

Along with this new information, I was also led to read a book titled *Discipline While You Can* by James Dobson. This book taught me a lot about healthy parenting and setting boundaries. I followed his guide with all my children throughout their developmental years as best I could.

I firmly believe that Jesus visited our house that night and through that visit we were led to get the right help for our son. His personality changed overnight and his behaviour improved a great deal. The main challenge was to get others to understand that there were certain foods he could not tolerate. Poor Benjamin got pretty sick of carob Easter eggs over the years but we learned not to give him chocolate as a 'monster child' would soon emerge if we did.

Before long our second son, Andrew, arrived, and from the moment he was born he was such a placid baby. I was so relieved to have a less active son. He brought peace with him and I've always referred to him as 'my healing baby'. He certainly brought a special love with him. Benjamin adored having a younger brother and even though they went through the usual sibling rivalry, they grew up to be good friends.

Coming from a family of five brothers, I so longed for a daughter, and before long I was pregnant with my third child. During my pregnancy I confided in my father how much I wanted a daughter because I had had years of football, guns and spiders. During my pregnancy I was too scared to find out the gender of my child and decided that whatever I had would be a gift from God and would be much loved, regardless of gender.

My birth with Julia went very well and was ever so fast. I seemed to cope well apart from getting sick of hearing the midwife referring to my new baby as a boy before she was born. When Julia was born I phoned my father and I told him I had a wee baby girl, we both burst into tears at the same time. It was a magical moment.

I really enjoyed having a new baby girl and dressed her immaculately. Even at three months of age she was taken to church in a pink frilly dress. I somehow managed to pin gorgeous ribbons in her hair even though she had very little hair to pin them into. Julia seemed to be a very happy, independent little girl who knew her own mind, enjoyed life and looked up to her big brothers.

I had my family, three beautiful children, and was hoping to live happily ever after. Sadly this was not to be. I found it hard to have three young children. I became quite depressed and tearful, and had no idea what was wrong with me when I could not stop crying. One night I was up until all hours sobbing and Thomas said, 'Kerry what is the real problem here? You can tell me.' I honestly did not know what was worrying me, but then something very deep inside myself came out and I said, 'I am nearly thirty and I still feel like a little girl inside. I don't feel like a grown-up.' Thomas smiled and said, 'That's OK because I'm thirty and I still feel like a little boy inside, and that's OK.' It was like he was giving me permission to just be me.

Thomas was a very kind man and a good father to my children. He took good care of me. From the outside no one would ever see trouble brewing in our marriage. We did struggle financially, and I forced myself to be a domesticated, stay-at-home mother. I just wanted to break free to be me and looking back, maybe being a working mother would have suited me better. I loved my children to bits but staying at home being a housewife seemed to lull me into depression.

As a child I had decided quite clearly that when I was a grown-up and a mother, my house was going to be always clean and tidy. I would provide home-baking for my family, serve lovely meals at the dinner table and always have scrumptious lunches. I rarely experienced this growing up as my childhood home was very disorganised. My birthday is in early January and my mother decided this was a good reason to never have a birthday party, birthday cake or wrap a lovely present for me on my birthday. It was more of a case of 'Look in the cupboard and you will find something there for your birthday.' So when I had children of my own, we made both Christmas and birthdays very special and we opened presents together and always celebrated every birthday with a party and a cake.

When I attended Thomas's work Christmas function every year, the other wives talked about their work and all the exciting things they were up to, and I had nothing to talk about but my children and kindergarten and nappies. I was so bored with my life! The next day we went to the park with a picnic and I started sobbing and said to Thomas, 'I think you should divorce me, I am such a boring person.' He could not understand how I could think like that.

Not long after that one of my sisters-in-law started working part-time as a nurse, and I decided that would be a great thing for me to do. I started working on weekends and sometimes in the evening and suddenly I felt so much happier! My smile came back and I enjoyed my family so much more. I even saved enough to take the family on a holiday to Australia. My husband said it was happiest he had ever seen me.

## *Change kicks in*

Our family hummed along quite well for a while. We made friends with our neighbours and started socialising together. Something was missing in my marriage and I often wondered if being married was something I had been told to do rather than something I truly wanted. I found intimacy difficult because of my past and I am sure this didn't help. My husband dearly loved me and was such a good man, yet I had conflicting and confusing feelings about him and our marriage. When I look back now, I often encourage people to work through things in their marriage rather than running away, because as my son said to me in his adult years, 'It's not a broken marriage, it's broken children.'

I continued my nursing at a new nursing home and met new friends there, and also decided to become an aerobics instructor! Somehow I managed to achieve this too, as well as playing netball with other mums.

Thomas was never that happy with his job and wanted to work for himself, so I encouraged this. He started working as a sub-contractor, and then I started working as a part-time advertising salesperson, as I had decided to have a change from nursing. I really enjoyed the challenge and excitement of work and eventually ended up working full-time, while Thomas took a back seat, working part time and cooking the family's evening dinners. The new friends I had met wanted me to go out to nightclubs and have fun with them. At first I was completely shocked at the thought of going out without my husband but before long I started going out by myself with my friends and drifting away from my marriage.

Then one dreadful evening I received a phone call from the abuser from my childhood. Something snapped inside me and I broke down. Here was this man phoning me, who had sexually abused me for years, asking for sympathy about something that had happened to someone close to him. I felt he was a complete hypocrite and I couldn't believe he thought it was perfectly acceptable to phone me for sympathy!

My husband tried to console me but I was so confused. I ended up phoning my parents in desperation to ask for their help and to confide in them about what had happened to me. My father completely swept the whole thing under the carpet, totally denying what had happened to me as a little girl. I reached out to them with my heart asking for their understanding, acceptance and support, only to be rejected. I was told that I was the one who had the problem.

I will never fully understand what came over me but I decided I had to end my marriage. These years were very dark and sad, and the grief was immense. My parents completely disregarded what had happened to me as a child, like I was imagining things. According to them, none of what I told them could possibly have happened. It was a huge act of denial from my parents. I know Thomas offered to talk things through with me and I know he truly cared but something was driving me forward.

Anyone who has been through a broken marriage when there are children involved knows just how painful it all is. Broken dreams, promises and hearts, and the children often get hurt and caught up in the middle. This is why I often advise and encourage marriages to stay together if they can when there are children involved because sometimes I believe things can be saved and turned around. Escape is not the only option.

Whenever I looked at Thomas all I could see was his hurt and confusion. I knew I had broken him and I didn't know what to do. The guilt was immense. Along with this I also grieved because I wasn't with my children all the time any more. My lawyer put my mind at rest when she said to me, 'Kerry, you will never lose your children. No matter what, you will always be their mum.'

I felt bewildered after the break-up in the early days. Driving to work one day I saw three rainbows in the sky and somehow I knew everything was going to be OK. I knew this was a sign from God letting me know that all was in hand. In the first few weeks I nearly went back to my marriage because the pain was too much to bear.

In fact there were three times that I nearly went back to my marriage but for some reason I was stopped each time. It was like there was some other plan for me. On one occasion I was going to a friend's house for dinner one Friday night. I announced to her that it was all too much and I was going to go back to my marriage. She said, 'Just pause. Is there any hurry?'

It was my turn with the children that night. When I saw Thomas I just knew I couldn't go back so I didn't say anything. We had agreed that I would sleep in the main bed and he would sleep on the couch that night. Just being with my children and having a beautiful warm bath and sleeping in peace, I felt whole again.

The next evening I was due to go out with a friend for the night. I was feeling quite refreshed for the first time since my marriage had broken up. We headed into a nightclub in the city

— I felt so free, dancing and being myself. I took a break from dancing and was sipping on a glass of lime and soda when a man whispered in my ear 'Would you care for this dance?' I looked up at a young Englishman with dark, floppy hair who reminded me of Hugh Grant. We danced the night away, trying to make conversation over the loud music.

It wasn't too long before he told me he was only 23 years old. I was aghast because I was 32, but said to myself, 'Who cares if I date this guy? I can't get married for another two years at least so give him a go.'

Romance blossomed and to be honest I feel this is the first time that I properly fell in love in my life. When I look back, if I had not met Daniel when I did I most likely would have gone back to my first husband. It was a stroke of fate that prevented me from going back there.

Daniel and I moved in together. I knew my family would completely flip out once they knew — not only had I left my husband, but I was living in sin with a younger man! Oh my goodness, you just don't do that sort of thing in a Catholic family. I did it anyway.

## *Picking up the pieces*

My feelings were all over the place: I was grieving for my marriage, the happy family we once were and especially for the way my children had been affected by our breakup. I felt guilty for falling in love with a new man when I was still letting go of another. I honestly didn't know what to do. Daniel encouraged me a lot over those years, helping me to understand the little girl Kerry as well as the woman. I began to accept myself as a woman for the first time. He brought something to me that I had never experienced before. I started to heal.

Daniel was amazing with my children. He would really get down to their level; he knew how to relate to them so well and we had a lot of fun together. He had an incredible imagination, which encouraged me to feel like a child again and to see things through children's eyes. At the same time the children were so sad about the marriage breakup — one thing I have learnt from having a broken marriage is to never put down or blame the other parent as it only affects your children. Even though my children enjoyed Daniel they also felt disloyal to their father.

Mum, most of my brothers and my aunts and uncles completely rejected me over this time, and I was basically kicked out of my Catholic family. I was the evil witch and Thomas was the saint. Dad did keep in touch with me over this time, as did one of my brothers. When family celebrations came up I was never invited, including my mother's seventieth birthday. It hurt a lot to be rejected by my family and judged so harshly. Looking back I can see how mixed up I was and that I hadn't dealt with abuse from my past. In later years when I became a celebrant, I learnt that 'grief is one of the most consistent and loyal of all companions'. If not dealt with it will catch up with you. In my case it certainly did.

Even now, I can still remember the phone call from my father telling me that he had been diagnosed with oesophageal cancer and that he was determined to overcome it. I choked up with pain. I didn't want to lose Dad and I didn't know how I would live my life without him. He seemed to cope well with the cancer and kept himself busy, so the reality of cancer did not hit any of us at first. One morning I had a phone call from my dad and I knew instantly he would not have long on this earth. He had become very religious in later years and went to church every morning at St Mary's Church in Northcote. On this morning he was blinded by the sun and pulled out in front of another car, which went straight into him. From my nursing experience I knew that if a cancer patient received shock or trauma like this it could speed up the cancer.

My father went downhill and I spent as much time with him as I could. I would visit my parents' house and ignore Mum as best I could so I could spend time with Dad. Mum found it hard to cope with my father's illness and he was admitted into North Shore Hospice where I visited him frequently. He begged me to get my marriage with Thomas annulled so I could re-marry in the Catholic Church. I sobbed in my father's arms begging for his forgiveness for the pain I had caused him. He just held me and appeared to understand.

Before my father became really ill, Daniel and I had planned and paid for a trip to the UK to visit his home and to catch up with his father in Italy. Dad was still alive and I decided to cancel my trip to the UK because I knew I still needed to be there to spend as much time with him as I possibly could. I decided not to try to organise events and just to let the angels, God and the universe deal with it.

My father passed away before we were to leave for the UK and I was devastated. In some ways it pulled the family together and I was accepted back in just a little bit. A few members of the family cruelly blamed me for my father's death. I guess I was a scapegoat for their grief.

The day after my father's funeral, my divorce was due to go through and so I met Thomas at the district court in Takapuna. It was one ending after the other. Thomas's words to me were, 'I was there at the beginning, I may as well be there at the end.' The divorce went through quickly and we then went out for coffee and had a chat. It seemed like the obvious thing to do. It was the first time I was totally honest with Thomas about how I felt.

Daniel and I left for the UK and Italy as planned. I was still grieving of course, and I knew it was too much for Daniel to completely understand what I was going through. When I arrived in the UK I had a sense that I had been there before. It was like a feeling of coming home. Italy was fun as well but at times the tears would come from nowhere. The grief just wells up inside you and you have no choice but to allow yourself time to grieve. I can remember feeling angry that Dad never really travelled. He would have loved to have seen the architecture, buildings and history in Italy. Little did I know he was actually with me when I was having these thoughts and feelings.

It is interesting in life how unexpectedly we can let go of something and be healed when we least expect it. This happened on my trip to Italy. As we visited historic places, I started to feel overwhelmed with all the paintings of heaven and hell and how frighteningly hell was portrayed. My buttons were being pushed because of my religious upbringing and my family's disapproval at me 'living in sin'. As we walked into a church in Florence, I noticed that the entrance was covered in art of heaven and hell and eternal damnation. Fear rose fiercely inside me and when we went upstairs to view the dome I broke down in tears. Daniel was a very compassionate young man; he asked me to share what was worrying me so I blurted out 'We are living in sin, I know I am going to hell,' and pointed at all the art we had been viewing. He burst out laughing and said to me, 'Kerry, look up on the ceiling, there is a devil poking a hot poker up someone's bottom. It's a cartoon.' I laughed too and suddenly understood that the best way to control another person is through fear, and this is how I had been controlled most of my life.

Not long after the trip to the UK Daniel and I became engaged to be married. I was over the moon. However, deep down it was too much for Daniel and he started to have doubts that he could follow through with his commitment. At the same time I was still grieving over my marriage and the loss of my family unit and my darling dad. I was insecure about our age difference and could not cope with the wrinkles and grey hair that had started to appear. The mixture of Daniel being not ready for commitment and my insecurity and unresolved grief ensured the relationship was doomed.

Sadly Daniel ended our relationship and I am sure it hurt him as much as it hurt me. He had become my rock, I honestly felt I had nowhere to turn. This is when my whole life headed in a completely new direction that I could never have imagined.

# 13

## *Break down to break through*

When I broke up with Daniel the sun did not shine any more. I felt empty, cold, lost and alone.

My marriage had finished, my father had passed and now the man I thought was the love of my life had vanished. Three significant endings in three years — looking back I can see how much I was in a state of grief at the time. Grief is like being lost in mushy soup; you cannot seem to find your way out even if you try.

I learnt a lot about grief in those years, such as how much it hurts when people make sweeping statements. For example, when someone has passed over: 'At least he is out of pain now.' 'He is in a better place now.' 'He lived a good life at least.' 'At least he lived a few years longer than others.' 'Things could be worse, there is always someone worse off than you.'

When people say these sort of things they are telling you to zip your grief up and put it away. Fix-it advice only makes the grieving person feel a lot worse.

It's the same when someone is going through a significant relationship break-up. When I broke up with Daniel, I was told: 'Better now than later.' 'Don't worry, I feel he didn't really love you.' 'Plenty more fish in the sea.' 'At least you didn't have any children with him.' 'At least he was honest with you.' I think the statement that hurt me the most when Daniel and I broke up was 'better now than later'. I was engaged to be married, excited about our wedding and felt totally rejected and hurt when people said those types of things. How could they be so cruel with their well-meaning, thoughtless statements?

When someone is hurting or in grief, I feel empathy is the best thing for them to hear. 'I hear you.' 'It must be hard.' 'I am thinking of you.' Often it's a good idea to offer someone who is grieving practical support as they are often walking around in a haze. Practical tasks may be too hard for them at the moment. Another important thing is not to judge, but just listen.

People also may avoid people who are grieving as they are embarrassed and do not know what to say. I personally found it was better to have my grief acknowledged — not fixed — and for people to listen — not judge — and show empathy.

After Daniel left I felt as if I was just going through the motions in life. I would wake up in the morning feeling it was just another day to endure. It was hard when I saw people around me happy and full of joy, I think I felt guilty that I could not enjoy and embrace life like they did.

Around this time, my children Julia and Andrew were asked to play the parts of Joseph and Mary in a Christmas parade. Usually when the children dressed up in fancy dress for a show, I would hire or buy something special so they looked the part. This time I couldn't face it, and I found a few things at home instead. Memories flooded back to me of when I was a child dressed in a sheet as an angel, and I had to wonder if my mother was grieving or depressed at the time. She did not have the energy to look after me how I needed to be looked after. I felt a lot of guilt as a mum at this time.

I had bought a house on the North Shore after my divorce,

but now decided that I didn't want the house any more, so I sold it. I broke all the Catholic rules and phoned a psychic from the Yellow pages. Looking back he was a very good psychic; he advised me to keep the house as I would regret it later on and my finances would be affected. I vowed at the time I would never go to a psychic again. Interestingly, how right he turned out to be, but we all have free will and I was simply not ready to listen.

I decided to move into my mother's house instead. This was the worst possible move I could have made. I also decided I needed some time off work and I should fly to Australia to spend some time with a friend, Jenny, in the Gold Coast. I intuitively knew that my life would be changed by this visit to Australia.

It was wonderful to see Jenny again, as I had not seen her for many years. Even though I was heartbroken over Daniel, I ended up speaking a lot with her about my first marriage to Thomas. Jenny is always such a happy and positive person, a woman after my own heart. She loves dressing up, adores fashion, and embraces being a woman and her feminine side. She is also very sensitive to spirit like me, but tends to the more religious, Christian side of things.

Even though Jenny was generally a happy person, I could sense that things were not as great in her life as they had once been. She was going through doubts about her own marriage so I did my best to encourage her to stay in her marriage and seek counselling for them both. She took my advice and went ahead with counselling, which thankfully worked and they stayed together. Despite my own marriage break-up I seemed to be able to help others going though marriage struggles, I always did my best to encourage people to stay together and seek help as I knew just how hard it was for everyone, especially for the children when a marriage ends.

Sometimes in life we experience a couple of days that we will never forget. The next two days were like that for me. I had been shopping with Jenny and bought some wonderful lipsticks and perfume. A little retail therapy often helps! I had $500 cash in my handbag, an awful lot of money 20 years ago. We decided to get some fresh air on a walk at 'The Spit', and I made the silly decision to put my handbag in the boot of her car for safety. On our return to the car I had a feeling something was amiss, I just knew it — and sure enough, my handbag containing all my money and new make-up had been stolen. Fortunately I had left my passport at Jenny's house.

I felt devastated to have had my handbag stolen with all my cards, driver license and holiday cash. Sometimes when you're down, life can throw you even more setbacks to overcome. However I have discovered that often at our lowest and darkest time in life, things can change forever in a very good and significant way. It is like the tide is out and just at the lowest ebb, it all turns around. A blessing in disguise.

If my handbag had never been stolen from the car that afternoon I may have never ended up where I am today.

# 14

## *My life will never be the same*

I needed to arrange a new credit card and prove that I had cashed my travellers' cheques, so the next day I headed to the bank at the shopping centre where I had cashed my travellers' cheques the day before. While I was queuing at the bank I experienced a terrible stabbing pain in my lower abdomen on the right-hand side. I thought there was something seriously wrong with me. After getting the proof I needed that I had cashed my traveller's cheques, I headed off to meet up with Jennifer. I was feeling so cold, the pain in my lower abdomen was excruciating and I was bent over in severe pain, not quite sure where I was going and with no way to contact anyone. I didn't even have Jennifer's home number on me. This felt like one of the lowest points of my life. My father had passed away, my marriage was over, Daniel and I had broken up, my handbag had been stolen and here I was in a foreign country, freezing cold, walking along the road doubled up in pain and feeling lost and completely alone.

Then I felt Elizabeth by my side. I had not felt her with me for many years and I instantly knew I was going to be OK. I could feel her directing me and giving me strength. I could not see or hear her as I had in the past, but I could feel the warmth of her energy. It was the most comforting feeling ever.

Things started to fall into place. American Express said I needed to wait a little longer for my card but directed me to a doctor in the mall. The receptionist was just lovely, and said the doctor would still see me and I could pay later once I had my new card. The doctor examined me and said because I had been coughing so much I had pulled a muscle in my stomach and that it was not too much to worry about, which was a big relief. I knew that there was something or someone looking after me, I could just feel it.

My card was ready and as I headed back to the doctor's to pay, it felt like my head was turned to the right. I saw a lady inside with rainbow-coloured hair sitting in a shop. I was intrigued by the way the lady had coloured her hair as rainbows were such a strong sign to me that all would be well.

In the corner of the room there was a lovely older lady doing readings. She looked very kind. I asked the lady with the rainbow-coloured hair if I could have a reading and she nodded and offered to make me a cup of tea while I waited. She handed me a book titled *Women Who Love Too Much* — it was like she could look right through me and see who I was. Even though I had decided I would never have a reading again, it felt like fate had brought me to this place.

I started to feel so guilty, daring to get a reading and go against my Catholic upbringing again. What a bad person I was! What would my mother think? Maybe I would be sent straight to hell for doing such a thing.

Even though I had all these thoughts welling up inside, I knew I had to have a reading with this very kind lady called Mary. I sat opposite her and she looked into my eyes and said, 'You are broken-hearted at the moment, but he will be back.' She then said,

'Daniel will be back.' She actually said his name. She said it would be about this time next year that we would be together again and he would ask me to marry him again.

Then she confused me by asking 'Who is John and who is Theresa?' I had no idea who these two people were but little did I know that they were to be very significant people and names in the future. Often as a psychic medium I may give information or names which my sitter does not always understand, and it is often something they have forgotten or something that has not quite occurred yet in their lives.

I felt over the moon at this reading, I just wanted to jump for joy! I headed back to Jenny's as soon as I could, feeling full of happiness and wanting to share this reading with her. When I shared the information with Jenny, she went very quiet and did not really want to talk about it due to her religious beliefs so of course I had to respect this.

On my return to New Zealand the weather was cold and gloomy. My mother was so difficult to be around. Despite the wonderful time and a positive reading in Australia the clouds came in around me and I had to face the reality of grief, loss and being alone. My children came to stay regularly which was wonderful; I was always much happier and at peace when I was with them.

One wet Friday night things turned very black for me. I felt I had hit rock bottom in my life and I honestly didn't want to live any more. My children were there as well and my mother was having a real go at me about something unnecessary. It was all too much to take and something inside me just snapped. I lost control, went up to her face and shouted at her, 'I hate your fucking guts.'

My mother looked at me with her mouth wide open, and took a step backwards in complete shock. I don't know what my poor children were feeling to have witnessed this scene between their own mother and grandmother. Time stood still. I didn't know what to do with myself, so I put the children calmly to bed and told them everything would be OK.

I went downstairs and sat in my father's study. The rain was pounding down, it was a dark, dismal night and I have never felt so low in all my life. I could never understand why people would contemplate suicide but these terrible thoughts of taking my own life came over me. I thought that slitting my wrists would be the easy way out and I could get rid of all the pain I was feeling.

I knew I needed help quickly. I grabbed the phone and called Lifeline; I cannot remember the conversation exactly but I can remember the counsellor explaining I could get assistance from the Help Foundation, which offered counselling and psychotherapy to victims of sexual abuse.

Around this time, I caught up with an old friend, Louise, and told her about my psychic reading in Australia. We had never discussed this subject before and I didn't know if she would be interested. Louise excitedly told me about an amazing woman called Maria who did readings. She lived on the North Shore and both Louise and her sister had visited her.

I visited Maria for a reading, and this experience was quite different. Very soon after beginning, she told me that my father had passed over and that he wanted to speak with me. She said he was sorry that he did not understand when I tried to tell him about the sexual abuse I had suffered. I was very confused and asked how my father could be here now, as he was dead. She explained that my father's spirit was there and he was speaking of the sexual abuse I had experienced when I was young. Over and over again my father apologised that he was not there for me.

Dad also said that when he was alive the reason he wanted me to go back to my first marriage was because he wanted to keep me safe, but now he understood that was not the right thing for me to do. He also said that Daniel would come back to me. Along with this he said, 'Your insides are all mixed up and need sorting.' This statement completely threw me as I thought he meant I needed an operation. Maria laughed and said, 'No he means your emotions and mind; you need help to sort yourself out.' He also said, 'The sooner you get on your bike and sort yourself out, the sooner Daniel will be back.' The next day a lady called Jean from the Help Foundation contacted me and asked if I could come in and meet with her. Seeing Maria was a totally life-changing experience. The power of mediumship not only helps grief but it can also guide you towards a journey of healing yourself.

# *The healing journey begins*

After seeing Maria, my life changed completely. I returned to see her over and over again, fascinated by the whole experience. I remember at one point the tape recorder kept stopping and starting and she just laughed, saying, 'Spirit is certainly letting themselves be known to us.' It was such an incredible experience; I couldn't get enough of it.

In her first reading for me, Maria said, 'You are a medium, just like your mother.' I was shocked. I had no idea that I was a medium and I certainly never thought of my mother as being a medium because she was so deeply religious. Although, she did used to speak in tongues and give prophecy, which I have since learnt is a form of mediumship, channelling what the Catholics refer to as 'The Holy Spirit'. Spiritualists speak of the same spirit energy; it is all the same source, just different names.

Maria suggested to me that I learn and develop myself as a medium. She led a group of people who were working to develop their skills. I thought this was a great idea and eagerly joined her group one Friday evening. I was expecting alternative, hippy types, and searched through my wardrobe to hunt out my weirdest, most colourful clothes.

On arrival I was shocked to see a group of very decent, normal-looking people. I felt out of place in my strange, uncoordinated clothes. I remember two very smartly dressed woman in suits, with beautifully groomed hair and make-up, who spoke well and looked very professional. I was happy to discover that everyday people were interested in this type of thing.

Learning about mediumship just blew me away. Discovering meditation and seeing auras for the very first time was incredible. One night Maria asked me to stand up and face the wall, and she said someone was going to stand behind me. She asked me to tell her about the person who was there. I felt a tall lady with fair hair and described her to the group. Maria asked what she was wearing and I replied that she was wearing a watch. 'What colour is the strap?' asked Maria. In my mind's eye I could clearly see a white watch-strap but my logic kicked in and told me I couldn't possibly know. I started listing colours: black, blown, silver, gold and so on. Maria could see what was going on and said, 'You know what colour the watch-strap is; you're just too scared to say it.' I whispered, 'White.'

Everyone clapped and laughed, and I had a huge feeling of relief. This was one of my biggest lessons as a psychic medium. Our logic often kicks in and takes over. Instead of giving what we see, hear or feel, our minds start guessing what the answer should be. That is where we go wrong.

Maria taught us to put our logic at the back of our mind and just give what we receive. After we have done this, we can then bring the logic back and analyse the information given to us. She said that we need to always do this whenever we are working with spirit and in meditation. When I am doing a reading I am always challenged by my mind questioning information I am receiving. Instinctively we want to do the best job we can, getting it right for the people we are doing readings for.

Meanwhile, I made my first appointment with Jean at the Help Foundation and my healing journey began. She told me at my first appointment that it was going to take a long time and I needed to persevere. She taught me a lot about boundaries as I had to arrive on time and when we were near the end of our session she would look at the clock and say, 'We have five minutes to go.'

Jean and I met frequently, and together we unwound the web of my life. This counselling and psychotherapy was long overdue. She also taught me about re-parenting myself and talking to my inner child. I felt myself feeling fuller inside.

My pining for Daniel never stopped, and I also felt a continuous aching in my stomach. I know now this was my solar plexus — the energy centre of personal power. As a child I recall getting butterflies in my stomach when I was nervous or feeling sick. Often when we are heartbroken, or going through grief, it is in our stomach that we feel it the most. It was a double-edged sword. Being told Daniel was coming back meant a huge part of me was holding onto hope and the other part of me was telling me to let it go and move on with my life. A state of limbo is not a nice place to be, feeling like your life is on hold because someone is supposed to be part of it.

Daniel and I would catch up from time to time, but he never gave me any indication that he wanted to be back together. I had become a bit addicted to psychics, hoping every time that they would tell me what I wanted to hear. If they told me what I wanted to hear I rated them highly. I now know how it feels when a client is pressuring you to give them something that they desperately want to hear.

I regret that my children saw me go through this 'crazy psychic Mum stage'. In their eyes they see my spiritual work as being for divorced people with problems and that is not what it is about at all. It would have been wonderful to have brought them up knowing and understanding the spirit world. Saying that, everyone has their own beliefs and I have to respect that.

I remember asking myself how I would feel if Thomas, my ex-husband, met another woman. Not long after I had these thoughts that is just what occurred. One Sunday afternoon I was driving over to the North Shore to drop off my children and, much to my surprise, Thomas came and met me in the driveway and told me he had a lady friend he would like me to meet. I quickly reached into my purse and found my lipstick because there was no way I was going to meet his new lady without having my lippy on.

After a cup of tea and a chat, I felt perfectly comfortable and ready to leave. I was so happy and relieved that Thomas had met someone new. Driving along in the car, I was yelling out, 'I'm free, I'm free, I'm free.' At long last I could let go of my burden of guilt, as I felt deeply sad that I had hurt Thomas so badly. I was happy that he was now free to love someone else. It was a feeling of 'breaking free' and it felt so good.

Many years later I realised that the name of the lady he married was the exact name that the psychic had given me, back in Australia.

I continued developing both my psychic and mediumship skills, and then one day I met up with a girl I used to go to school with at Carmel College. Her name was Amanda and I had been in the same class as her younger sister. Amanda and I had frequently bumped into each other over the years. We had our babies around the same time and two of our sons became very good friends for a while. When I saw her in the supermarket I told her about all my experiences and about the medium Maria, who had been teaching me. She seemed intrigued.

Before long Amanda was also coming along to meditation classes with Maria, and we became the best of friends over this time. She was having marriage difficulties and also had children to consider. I encouraged Amanda to stay with her husband and work it out as I knew how difficult it is to go through a broken marriage, but she made the decision to separate. We were both being driven forward to live a new life and develop spiritually.

I decided to buy a new house, and found a lovely three-bedroom house in Pakuranga. It was number 23; the number of the house added up to five, which is often about finding balance and having a good social life, and this is indeed the case. I had various flatmates, quite a few parties and a lot of fun, and started to heal. My children came and stayed with me a great deal, and I spent as much time with them as I possibly could.

Spring was coming, I felt a lot happier and I remember going for many happy walks around my new neighbourhood. One of these mornings as I was walking along, I had the biggest and deepest sense of knowing that I had ever experienced. I knew Daniel would be back. This is called claircognizance. My anxiousness about Daniel returning just left me and I felt a wave of peace move in.

Very soon after this Elizabeth started speaking to me again. When I was a child, she looked like a child as well, but now she came with a new fresh energy with long, black, wavy hair and a beautiful long white gown. She told me that I had a lot of work to do and many people to help in my life, and that Daniel would be part of my life but not all of my life.

I decided at this time to purchase tarot cards and a pendulum, and started teaching myself how to use them. I also did a chakra-balancing course, which was a lot of fun. I started to pick up more and more on spirit through my work with Maria, and Amanda and I often compared notes.

The early stages of spiritual development are often the most exciting because it is all so new and fresh; there is so much to learn. Amanda and I used to go to local psychic fairs together, marvelling over the crystals. We met many people interested in the spiritual arena and enjoyed getting to know them.

Daniel started making a bit more contact with me at this time and we would see each other occasionally. I held out hope but not in such a desperate way, and I also started dating different men at this time. For some reason I seemed to attract a lot of people into my life over these years and made many new friends. It was like I was forming a new life all over again.

At one point I went to Sydney for a work conference, and formed good friendships with some of the people there. I ended up contacting Daniel, telling him what a great time I was having in Australia and how he would love the whole experience. One evening I returned to the hotel from a night out to find a message waiting: 'See you for dinner tomorrow night. D x'.

My heart was pounding like mad! I couldn't believe that Daniel was coming over to see me. How romantic! I couldn't wait; my imagination went wild! Daniel arrived the next evening as promised. We were going out to a formal dinner with my work colleagues and fortunately Daniel brought a suit with him.

Sometimes in life we come out with the most stupid comments. Once you've said it, that's it — you've said it. No matter what you do, you can never take those words back again. I had been spending time with a work colleague who wore the most amazing suits. Daniel was all dressed up in his grey suit feeling quite good about himself, when I said, 'I think we need to get you a new suit, that one looks a bit old fashioned.' Daniel's face showed his disbelief and hurt. If only I could have wound back the clock.

# *Time away brings change*

At this time in my life my girlfriends and I often went away for fun weekends together. I remember a weekend away with Amanda, where we talked and talked about spiritual things the whole time. In particular we were convinced that the Pink Terraces in Rotorua were incredibly spiritual.

On the way home we stopped at a psychic fair to see what interesting things we could discover. Of course I decided to have a reading, but unfortunately it was a dreadful experience. I've since learnt that you have to be so careful when getting a reading because in some ways you are giving your power away to another person. If you have a reading with someone and you feel devastated afterwards, very often the reading is not correct.

The reading with this lady was awful. She told me Daniel was with a woman he loved much more than me and he would never come back to me, that I was wasting my time and I simply needed to get over it and move on. Amanda reassured me that this reading was rubbish, and also suggested we call in and see Daniel on the way home.

Daniel was very surprised when he opened the door to two young ladies with bright smiles on their faces. He asked us in for a hot drink, and we willingly accepted the invitation. Daniel asked me if we could catch up soon, and Amanda noticed that his hands were shaking a little.

A little while later, I headed to Napier on a business trip. Daniel had been more and more on my mind. He called to ask if I would like to be picked up at the airport on my return and of course I said yes.

I was getting a bit edgy about the whole thing with Daniel. I wanted to say, 'Stop mucking me around, are you coming back or not?' At my meditation group Amanda said she felt my father around her and he told her that it was important that I take some deep breaths, control myself and not to do anything as Daniel was about to come back to me. She said she saw my dad jumping around saying, 'Tell Kerry to calm down and don't do anything, Daniel is coming back.'

A few weeks after the Napier trip, Daniel was in touch again and we arranged a trip to the snow. I decided to be very quiet and not come out with any silly statements, as I had previously in Australia a few months before.

The trip to the snow was fantastic. We all had so much fun, and yes, Daniel and I reunited once again after 14 months of ups and downs, holding on and letting go.

Not long after we got back together I sold my house in Pakuranga, and we bought our first house together in Howick. Our intention was to live happily ever after. I had changed in the time we had been apart and had begun to develop my gift as a psychic medium. This was all new to Daniel, but he seemed more than happy for me just to be me and to keep progressing with it all.

I was over the moon to have Daniel back in my life. At first everything seem to go very well. Then he was approached to act in a play and even though I was happy for him to follow his acting passion, I knew there was going to be interference in our relationship. Warning bells went off in my head. He seemed to take an interest in one of the young girls in the play; he spent a lot of time with her and I felt quite insecure in our relationship. At social occasions I definitely got the vibes from her and in later years one of my friends confirmed to me that Daniel and this young lady had a common interest in each other.

We pushed forward with our relationship, having fun and adventures together. Daniel was the ideal stepfather for my children. Sometimes though when things are not dealt with properly, they rear their ugly face again. There were problems coming from both sides of our relationship.

The first problem was my insecurity about myself. Daniel was nine years younger than me, and I was concerned that as I aged, he would leave me for a younger woman. My body clock was ticking and I knew at 37 I didn't have a lot of time left to have children with Daniel. The second problem was that Daniel had a fear of commitment, because of his upbringing and his father's attitude against marriage. He found this very hard to deal with.

The opposite of fear is love. If we both had been strong enough to understand this then things may have been different. The love was there but the fear would turn out to be greater.

# A working medium

I was developing well as a psychic medium, doing readings with friends at first for a bit of fun. Many of my friends were so happy with the readings that they started telling their friends about my gift. News started to get out about my abilities and suddenly I found myself doing paid readings for friends of friends.

Daniel did not mind me doing readings. I would take clients off to a spare bedroom in the house where we would sit on the double bed together as I did my reading. I was well known as the psychic Kerry who does readings on the bed in the bedroom. Not exactly a professional set-up!

Being a medium is like being a telephone or the bridge between two worlds. I began to realise that I could never remember my readings. Later on in my development I became aware that good mediums often don't remember their readings as they are working with their creative mind and their psychic senses rather than their logical mind.

I can recall being told about one particular reading afterwards by the client, a lovely lady called Patricia, although I can't recall the reading itself. I told her she was going to England for a holiday; she confirmed that they were going in the next week or two. I warned her that her legs could swell up from the plane trip and she should soak them in salt water when she arrived. She did have swollen legs when she arrived in England, and when she soaked her feet in salty water, the swelling in her legs came right down.

I then told her that she was doing some research on where she had come from and looking into family records, which she confirmed. I said, 'I have your Great-aunt Mary Agnus here in spirit, who has come to join us.' Patricia knew absolutely nothing of Mary Agnus. I was convinced I had Mary's spirit with me so I went on with more information.

When I was a younger medium I was a bit more cocky with the information I gave. If someone couldn't take it, I didn't worry as I knew it was from spirit. In later years this cockiness has left me and I really like to make sure the evidence is correct and the sitter can usually confirm it in a reading. Maria had taught me to be confident and she used to say, 'Once you have given it you cannot take it back, you just give it and stay with it.' She told me to believe in the intelligence of spirit.

Even though Patricia could not confirm this extra information it didn't seem to faze me and I pushed on with it. Mary Agnus told me she lived to 95; she was the life and soul of the party and she was a widow as her husband had died very young. She also said she had shares in a famous English farm that was lost through the war. None of this information made any sense to Patricia at the time.

Patricia decided to investigate further into her family tree. She did indeed have a great aunt called Mary Agnus who lived to 95, and she was known as the life and soul of the party. She was widowed at a very young age and also said that the family had shares in Mayfair but the shares were lost because of the war.

Even though the first part of Patricia's reading made sense and the second half didn't, the fact that I had good evidence in the beginning proved that spirit was working with me. If a sitter cannot confirm the information at the time, they will often find out later that it is true.

Patricia visited me again just after her mother had passed away, and a similar thing happened. Most of the reading made sense but there was something she couldn't understand at the time. Her lovely mum came through and showed me an image of herself crossing the road carrying a white bag; apparently she had just bought some milk when she crossed the road and had been hit by a car. She then showed me a sapphire ring.

I told Patricia about this sapphire ring that belonged to her mother and that it was in a drawer in her bedroom of her house. Patricia and her father searched the house but found no trace of a ring. Three months later Patricia's father decided to move on from his home and removed the top drawer to pack, and a sapphire ring fell out. Patricia was over the moon to confirm that her mum was safe and had been communicating with her all along.

Grief is one of the hardest things in the world to deal with. I know that although mediumship cannot fix grief, it can help to ease the pain greatly and help us on the journey of our lives. To know that our soul is eternal and our spirit does live on, that we will see our loved ones again in the world unseen. The only way for people to truly believe this is for a medium to give such good evidence that is so individual to the person who has passed over that there is no room for doubt.

Over the years I have become very pedantic about my mediumship. I know how it is so important to give very good evidence of survival because unless you can give this it is not comforting to the sitter. If you get the link right and are able to give correct and good evidence about their loved one, they know that their loved one lives on and that they will indeed be seeing them again.

On one occasion I gave a reading to a lady who was so full of grief, she could hardly get out of bed and get on with her life. She was really struggling as her partner had committed suicide. Not long after the reading commenced her partner came through and the pain was very deep. He showed me his long hair, his tattoos, his guitar, even the type of guitar he played and she knew without a doubt this was him. He then told her it was not her fault but at first she did not believe this message.

He told me that he had a problem with depression and that he had attempted suicide twice before, which his partner confirmed. He then said he had a chemical imbalance in his brain for which he took medication, and he said, 'We had an argument before I did this'. Again, the sitter agreed that these facts were correct. He then said to me, 'Regardless of the argument I was still going to do it, it made no difference because this suicide had been planned.' It was so important for her to hear this for her own healing.

After this reading the lady was able to move on with her life and let go of the guilt that had been weighing her down for months. She saw a grief counsellor and started to rebuild her life once again. I knew after this reading that being a medium and helping people was indeed my soul's purpose; I did not need to look further for what I really needed to do in life.

More and more people started coming to me for readings and all of this was word of mouth. I could see the changes I was making in many people's lives.

I can still remember a lady called Julie who came to see me. I described a brother who was still living in the UK and she confirmed this. I saw him with a long stick reaching up to windows and she laughed and said her brother was a professional window-cleaner. Her mother's spirit told me that Julie was estranged from her brother and that she had not heard from him for 20 years, which was also correct. The mother then said something incredible: 'He sometimes loses his temper and he is sorry for this. You will hear from him very shortly.' Julie nearly fell off her seat and acknowledged that her brother did have a temper but she said there is no way he would ever contact her again.

Only one week later a very excited Julie phoned me to say that her brother had phoned her the previous night. He said he was so sorry for what he had done and it was entirely his fault. She could not believe it! He told her that he had a daughter and a wife and they would like to come to New Zealand and to reconnect with her once again. Julie was over the moon. She was convinced now that her mum's spirit had come through to her telling her this amazing information. She felt the spirit was full of love and healing, and was at peace. The magic of spirit never ceases to amaze me and I am always in awe of this great power.

Even though Daniel was not involved with my readings, he was open to me doing what made me happy. Since we had been apart I had gathered a whole new network of people around me and I had grown as a person. Many of my friends had an interest in spiritual work. I have realised over the years to be successful in whatever you do in life, it is important to have a good team of people behind you to support you and believe in what you do.

We had many social gatherings, parties and barbeques at our home in Howick, and lots of fun holidays together. I saw my children often; they would come and stay every second weekend and in the school holidays, and twice a week I would take them out for dinner. Seeing my children was such a highlight but I used to sob every time I took them home to their dad. Maria told me in one of our first readings together that my children would return to me and I would take care of them full time in the future. I was open to this, however even though Daniel loved my children, he was not sure about the full-time responsibility. At one point he suggested we shift to a different city and I said that I would never shift away from my children.

I had been told that there was a possibility of having two more children with Daniel, a girl and a boy. I liked to use the pendulum in those days and the pendulum always confirmed this as well.

It is never a good thing to pressure anyone in a relationship about further commitment unless they are ready. However, my body clock was ticking and time was running out for me to have another child. I felt like I was caught between a rock and a hard place.

# *Endings to bring new beginnings*

Daniel and I happily continued our relationship for a further two years and then I started making a lot of comments about marriage. After a while Daniel got the hint; one gorgeous afternoon he was playing a game with the children about finding things in people's ears and he went to my ear and lo and behold, there was a sparkly engagement ring. I was so excited.

On Monday nights I used to meet regularly with a group of friends interested in psychic work and mediumship. One of the girls came up with the name 'coven' so every Monday night we would meet for our coven night to discuss our spiritual interests. Of course none of us were into witchcraft, it was just a fun thing to call our special nights together. We would share stories over bubbles and dinner, get the cards and the pendulum out and have a lot of fun. We really did support each other a lot during those years.

Over the next few months I started planning our wedding but something inside told me that Daniel was not totally committed to what we were doing. I could really sense something was wrong. Insecurity can manifest many things in our life and I went into a spiral of fear and anxiety. I made an appointment to see my psychotherapist again to see if she could help me through this. One thing that made me fearful was the fact that I was nine years older than Daniel.

Daniel seemed to be pulling away and our relationship began to fall apart. I was also protecting myself from being hurt again by him and I will forever be thankful for my wonderful friends who were so supportive of me at this time. The wedding was getting closer and I started to feel more and more worried about our future. Daniel seemed to be very depressed and I didn't know what to do. One dreadful afternoon I came home and I can still remember the feeling of a black cloud hanging over him. He told me that he did not know if he could marry me.

At the time I was working for a wonderful company and my boss understood what I was going through at home. I was supposed to be attending a Christmas lunch and I knew I could not do it. Daniel had gone away for the night and I had no idea where he had been. I called a psychic for advice; I still don't know if this was the right thing to do. While it's OK to seek guidance from a psychic they are not God. Sometimes their own opinions come into the reading.

In the past this psychic had always been very positive and supportive of my relationship and said it would work out. However this time I had explained to her what had happened and rather than give me a message from spirit, she gave me her own opinion: 'You should put the wedding on hold and not go through with it.'

I took her word as gospel and I decided I was going to suggest to Daniel to put our wedding on hold. At lunch time Daniel arrived with two big bunches of roses begging for my forgiveness, saying that he couldn't wait to marry me. I did not go with my own heart and instead I used the words the psychic gave me: 'Are you sure you want to do this?' It was all downhill from there. Having said that, Elizabeth's words also rang in my head:

'Daniel will be part of your life but not all of your life.' When I remembered these words I found some inner peace.

Later on Daniel told me that he had gone for a walk in the middle of the night around a golf course and even though he said he was not sure if he believed in God he said a prayer and asked for a sign. He said, 'If the sprinklers go on then I am supposed to marry Kerry.' At the end of his walk a sprinkler turned on and completely saturated him so he decided it was right for us to proceed with our wedding. As much as the sign spoke to him, he was obviously very unsure about committing to me fully.

People will often come to me for readings in regards to relationship advice and through my own experiences I have learnt that it is nobody's right to tell you what to do. The psychic I saw had been good in the past but her own bias came into it that time. This was not a message from spirit, it was her opinion. The lesson that was important here was that I repeated what someone else told me to say and not what my inner being and heart was telling me to express.

I have learnt a lot about relationships and the influences from outsiders, whether they are a friend, a family member or a psychic. We all have to take personal responsibility and make our own choices no matter what well-meaning advice is given to us at the time. If I had not spoken to the psychic, would the wedding have gone ahead and would we have been able to sort out our problems, or would it have been cancelled regardless of what the psychic had said to me? I know if I had not spoken to her, things could have been very different. At the same time it was obvious that Daniel had huge doubts about moving forward in regards to marriage.

I had flashbacks of when Daniel and I broke up the first time. I had let someone else determine my fate and little did I know, this would happen yet again further down the track. Lessons keep presenting themselves to us in life until we learn from them. My lesson was to make my own decisions in life and this was all about breaking free so I could be me. No matter what I choose in life I know that I can live with my own life choices and not blame or resent another for swaying me.

Friends tried to support me, but I found comments such as 'better now than later' and 'he obviously didn't love you' very difficult to hear. The most helpful person at that time was the Catholic priest who was going to marry us. He had dealt with such a lot of grief so he knew just the right thing to say. He confirmed that all the well-meaning but thoughtless comments from friends were hurtful and not helpful at all. One of my friends also phoned me two days after we had called off the wedding to tell me she had just got engaged — I was very happy for her but it was hard to put a false smile on my face while aching inside.

I felt I had been broken apart and did not know how to put myself together. I was drawn to visit a colour therapist, which I thought was a bit hocus pocus but I decided to give it a go. She shone a light on me and placed various coloured ribbons on different parts of my body. Her first comment to me was, 'You are all over the place, your energy is completely shattered.' I explained what had occurred and she said that made sense to her.

Not long after some regular trips to the colour therapist, things started to improve. I became centred again. I don't know how it worked but I know that it did and the results were fabulous.

Even though we did not follow through with our wedding plans, Daniel and I kept moving along for a while but something inside me struggled. It was like there had been too much hurt and upset, the damage had been done and some of my feelings for him had died. I was concerned for Daniel because his father had told him never to get married or have children. I knew Daniel was meant to be a father and told him, 'It's not about me being the mother of your children, it's about you and what is meant for you. It would be so sad if you never had at least one child of your own.'

After staying another year together we ended up parting on Easter weekend in April 2000. Interestingly this was the same weekend that my current husband's marriage separated as well, although of course I hadn't met him at that time.

Why did psychics, clairvoyants and mediums all tell me that Daniel and I would be together and that we would marry and have two children? Could they all be wrong? The answer is no, none of them were wrong. Even my own father in spirit told me the same thing through more than one medium. I believe this comes down to one thing: we all have the gift of free will. For whatever reason Daniel and I had the potential to marry and have two children, but we both changed that outcome through our insecurities, fears and decisions we made along the way. A reading can only offer potential. At any time a person can change their own path and change outcomes. We create our own destiny. I love this key principle of spiritualism: personal responsibility.

## *A fresh start*

I was not nearly as devastated this time as I was when Daniel and I first parted. I had my own set of frustrations with our relationship and I think we let our own insecurities get in the way.

A very good psychic cautioned me to be careful about what I said to Daniel, as we could easily be friends for the rest of our lives but I needed to be wise, act with discernment and not be too reactive. I so wish I had heeded her advice. Even though I know now I am meant to be with my husband John, and he is a big reason for me being where I am now, it would have been nice to have remained on good terms with Daniel.

Before long I bought a new property in Howick and started to get on with my own life. I needed some time on my own for about six months. It was an interesting experience as I had never lived completely alone before and it was a healing time for me. I felt spirit around me very strongly at this time and did many healing meditations over this time to ground myself again.

However, I had not adjusted to financially supporting myself as I had been used to two incomes for the past three years. When I first lived with Daniel we budgeted and managed quite well. By the time we got back together Daniel had set himself up as an osteopath in his own business so there were more funds for us to come and go on. I became used to a higher standard of living and so when I was on my own my budgeting skills had gone out the door.

Elizabeth came to me one night in my dreams. She told me that my children were at last returning to me. My daughter would return first to live with me, and because of my love she would blossom into the most beautiful flower, and become an incredible mother to her own children one day. Elizabeth said my sons would soon follow after and this was my time to really become a strong, loving mother in their lives and not to question myself so much. She said I would have my trials and tribulations, but the spirit world would be there to support me. She told me my children loved me deeply and not only as their mother but also as their true friend.

After about six months, my daughter Julia ended up living with me once again. We had a very special time together and it helped to make up for the time when she was younger and I had returned to work full time. Eventually I was able to enrol Julia in a local Catholic school in Howick; she appeared to make friends quite easily and seemed settled. She was very hungry over these years and seemed to need some time off school but I swore that she grew an inch a week over this time. It was like she needed a break for her body to grow and blossom and intuitively I allowed this because I knew it was what she needed. She was underweight when she first came to live with me, and I used to fill her lunchbox to the brim every day. One day she turned around to me and said, 'Mum I don't need such a big lunch any more.'

My relationship with my daughter grew stronger and the boys would come to stay with us often. Having the children with me mended a lot of pain in my heart. I was very concerned about my middle son's welfare at the time, and had an argument with

Thomas about this. We both went to see lawyers to fight for legal custody but decided to drop it as it was an expensive waste of time. We were better off making our own agreement.

Thomas took me aside one day when I went to pick the boys up from him to announce he was shifting to the South Island with his new wife and he wanted to take the children with him. I did not hesitate to stand up to him, which I had never truly done since our break-up. It was like a lioness rose up instinctively in me, protecting my cubs, as I roared at him, 'Nobody is taking my children off me.' He stood back with his eyes wide open as he had never seen this side of me before.

About this time I had met a new man called Todd. I had Julia living with me at the time. We all got on like a house on fire and he moved in with us shortly after this. Todd was a truck driver with not a lot of money, but that did not bother me as I was more interested in being with someone who cared about and loved me and who would be good to my children.

Not long after we moved in together it was decided that the two boys would move in with me as well. I was overcome with joy. I had turned 40 and I was certainly ready for this in my life. I can still remember the day I picked up my two sons from Thomas's house just after Christmas; I will never forget the gorgeous grins that shone on their faces from ear to ear.

Todd decided he was going to lay down the law with my children and gave them a lecture over dinner about his authority in the household. It was bit of a shame to be honest. I knew from that point on that this relationship would be short-lived, as nobody was going to stand between me and my children.

At the time I decided to rent out my house in Howick and rent a house in Northcote which was closer to both my sons' schools. Sadly my tenant cost me a lot of money. I had not been budgeting well; I didn't think I was overspending but all the little luxuries added up over time. I also made a decision that was not wise and took a one-off payment of $10,000 in lieu of ongoing child support from Thomas.

I started struggling financially. Todd seemed directionless in his own life. I started noticing outbursts of anger and he also seemed to have a gambling problem. I loved him but knew this relationship would not be healthy for me or one that I could consider long term.

Money was tight over this time so I started to do private readings at home on the weekends to give me a wee bit more money to come and go on. At the same time, I began to question all the psychic stuff. Was my mother right, was it all evil? I decided to do some research and visited about five Catholic priests around the Auckland area. Only one of the priests said what I was doing was wrong and it confirmed how I had been brought up, but funnily enough the other four priests did not feel the same way at all. One of them looked me directly in the eyes and said, 'God has given you a special gift. It's OK as long as you use it wisely, but never think you are God.' I will never forget his wise words.

Some people think psychic mediums can read a person's mind. This is so far from the truth. I cannot read people's minds, nor do I wish to. I have no interest whatsoever in other people's private business. I believe being a psychic medium is a God-given gift to be respected and appreciated. We are given information through our senses, what we see, feel and hear. We are given the information that the spirit world wish to give us or what is right for us to know.

At this time in my life I was so confused. Even though only one out of five priests was negative about my psychic work, he was the one I listened to the most. He sent me to meet with a Catholic married couple in South Auckland, who counselled me to get rid of all my spiritual pictures, ornaments, cards and books.

So here I was, a struggling single mother living with a boyfriend who contributed very little, going through all my possessions so that Todd could take them away to the local dump. I remember there was an amazing wizard I had purchased in Australia, and pictures of a unicorn and Native American Indians that I let go of at this time. Todd told me later that one of his friends did salvage the amazing wizard.

Just as I tried to walk away from my mediumship and psychic gifts, they became stronger and stronger. I did try to turn my back on my psychic life but it didn't work, it felt as if I was swimming against the current. I found life was harder without it and I also missed the extra income that I really needed over this time. There was nothing to be gained from turning my back on my gift and I found that the people that told me not to do this did not have my best interest at heart. My spiritual friends like Amanda and Alice were always there for me no matter what. Throughout my life I keep being given this personal message from spirit: 'Decide for yourself what is best for you.'

Things deteriorated further with Todd. The final breaking point came when he sided with a neighbour complaining that my son's car had woken her when he was leaving early for work one morning. Todd could never come between me and my children. My instinct to protect my young was so strong.

I ended up asking Todd to move out as I didn't like his outbursts around the children. It was very sad to say goodbye to him, however my love for my kids and their peace of mind was much stronger than what I felt for Todd. My children were happy I had put them first. This made them feel important, loved and supported. I know that teaching them to love themselves and to believe in who they are really boosted their self-confidence and helped them to blossom into the amazing people they are today.

My middle son Andrew had started to play up, and in

hindsight I was a bit too trusting and not really aware of what teenagers could get up to. I was determined not to let anything bad happen to him and I watched him like a hawk. People were full of well-meaning advice and told me just to forget about it and he would come right in time but I knew instinctively that I had to be right onto him. When I see parents now of teenage children I give them the same advice: 'Don't just let them go and hope they will be OK. You are the voice of reason and they need you to be strong for them over this time.' I don't regret my decision to be strong with Andrew over this period, to not allow him to get away with things that were harmful to him, even though he seemed to really detest me. I knew one day he would thank me for it, and in later years he did. He has turned out to be a successful, fine young man.

Benjamin, who had been a bit more of a challenging child when younger, seemed to change significantly at this time. While I know he got up to the usual teenage tricks, he never got himself into too much trouble. Sometimes the eldest son can fall into the position of father figure when there isn't a man in the house. Looking back, Benjamin matured pretty quickly and felt protective over me. This must have been hard for him, and I am forever grateful for his support over these years.

## *Money troubles*

Money became more of a challenge. I really hit rock bottom with no way of getting out of debt. I remember when I was very unwell and needed to see the doctor but had no money left in my account. I had no idea how I was going to get through the week.

I had been living in some kind of dream world when it came to money, relying on credit cards and my overdraft. Earlier on I had approached a real estate agent to see if I could sell my home in Howick but because I had borrowed against my mortgage to survive I now had negative equity in my home. What was I going to do? I phoned my mum and asked her to say as many prayers as she could to assist me. She seemed to like doing this as it was her way of helping me.

Somehow I pulled myself together and went to work the next day, only to get a phone call from the Tenancy Tribunal telling me my tenant was going to sue me if I did not get new carpet because of the smell of dog urine from a dog we had struggled to toilet train, even though we had had the carpets thoroughly cleaned. I phoned the bank manager sobbing and told him that I was going to go bankrupt. Luckily I had a new bank manager who was a lot more understanding than the previous one. He assured me he was not going to let me go bankrupt and he was going to give me a $5000 loan to pull me through. I managed to find some second-hand carpet at a good price and get the room sorted and even kept some money aside for extra costs.

People in my life started to emerge to help me along the way. I had never had a great relationship with my mother but through forgiveness I had let a lot of things go. I started to realise that she was human and had her own struggles to deal with in life. Life had not been easy for her with six children and a husband who worked long hours. I loved my father dearly but he had not been around enough to support my mother with the parenting. My mother may have been going through a form of depression and really did not know how to cope with it all. Not only did I start to forgive my mother, I started to understand more about what she had to go through in her life. My mother had started to become my best friend.

Going through tough times really changes and grows you as a person. I do believe challenges are humbling and give you inner strength.

Even though we held very different spiritual beliefs, I would often go to Mum with my problems and she would listen and pray for me many times. I would sometimes pray with her and could feel such a strong spiritual presence around her, I remember one instance when I saw a monk standing next to her, winking at me like he understood. The energy coming from my mother was immense and I knew she had a very powerful spiritual gift. She gave me strength through these times. What she lacked as a mother when I was growing up, she gave back to me in later years.

My younger brother, who had been angry at me for hurting my parents when I left my first marriage, also told me he had forgiven me. He realised it was not my fault. He could see how responsible I had become and how much I was growing as a person. We came back together after all these years.

Other family members also started to accept me more. I was pulled back into the fold once again. They could see how hard I was trying to be a mother and father for my three children, as well as the sole provider. At one point I was in an awful job, but when I phoned Mum to say I couldn't stand it any longer, she said, 'Kerry, stop right now and calm down. You cannot leave your job, you have three children to look after, feed and put a roof over their heads. Just get on with it. You have no choice.' She was right — there was no choice but to get on with it and do without. I just had to survive. As they say 'Tough times don't last, but tough people do.'

My eldest brother told me, 'Kerry, you actually know what it is like to be a man.' He explained that many men feel like I do because they are the provider for the family, and it is a huge responsibility as other's lives are dependent on them. He explained that often men can be in a job they really don't like but they stay so they can provide for the family.

Alice, a friend, really saved the day with her budgeting skills. I phoned her and confessed that I was in a really bad way and I had nowhere to go. I was working full-time with three teenage children and had even taken on two boarding students. Since then I have learnt that you can control money, it does not need to control you. If you respect money then it will respect you back. It is another form of energy.

Alice said to me, 'Bring all your bills to me; don't be afraid, I just need to know every one of your expenses so we can really find out where you stand.' I was so embarrassed and told her it was a complete mess and I would never be able to work it all out. I thought there was no way Alice could help me get out of this mess. However she was so insistent that she could help and I had reached rock bottom financially so I decided to give it a go.

In my experience I have found that people who get themselves in financial messes of their own doing often do not want advice. They are afraid that they may have to change, which can be frightening. We live in denial because of our fear of change, so we become stuck. Often this happens when people are under financial strain, because they are embarrassed. It is easier to pretend the problem does not exist rather than facing reality and dealing with it. Once you face your fears, often it is not as bad as you think.

So there we were over a cup of coffee, bills piled over the table as Alice started writing down all my expenses. I sat there with a huge knot in my stomach with my heart pounding in my chest. She seemed to be so calm and confident about what she was doing, and asked the tough questions. 'OK now Kerry, what can you do without?' I had to face up to myself, be honest and cross things off the list that were not necessary. She advised me to set up weekly automatic payments for things like power, phone, rates and school fees. I was given a budget of $150 a week to spend on my groceries, Pak 'n' Save became my biggest friend. Once all my bills had been paid I had $80 per week left over for all our clothes, children's activities, entertainment, all medical and health expenses, beauty expenses and the children's school requirements. Anything extra went to the children. From the bottom of my heart I will always thank Alice for being brave and kind enough to help me out at this time in my life. It takes courage to hold out your hand to another and the same courage to take the hand that is offered to you.

My mother was struggling financially at the time and could not help me, so the only person I had to rely on was me. The wonderful encouragement that friends and family gave me certainly helped and I know a higher power was always there, holding everything together.

I found working life quite a challenge. I had shifted back to Howick into my own home as it was less expensive to live there. Unfortunately it was more difficult for my sons having their friends based on the North Shore, so I changed Andrew's school to a public school in Pakuranga. His lovely, innocent personality seemed to change and, as teenagers do, he slowly became influenced by his peers. He told me that at his Catholic school on the North Shore he had to refer to his teachers as Sir or Madam, but at this new school he was laughed at for saying such things. He observed some children swearing at the teachers instead of treating them with respect. This was quite a shock to Andrew and I started to notice a change in my lovely sensitive boy.

Although my time as a single mum was very challenging, it strengthened me as a person. I grew from it, and formed a very strong bond with all three of my children and my mother. A lot of healing took place with important people in my life and I was accepted back into my own family.

Over this period I had two very powerful spiritual experiences that have stayed with me for life. In the middle of the night I was in a semi-waking state and I could feel a man hugging me ever so warmly and gently. It was incredibly comforting. I could physically feel his arms around me and thought my son had come in to give me a cuddle. I opened my eyes and could see a male figure cuddling me. He then let go and I heard the door open and he left. I immediately jumped out of bed as I was sure it must have been my Andrew but he was in a deep sleep. I felt that it was my father's spirit that had come to visit me in the middle of the night.

I decided to phone my mother in the morning to tell her about what had occurred the evening before and she went into a panic. Even though we were much closer than before, she was a very strict Catholic and would not tolerate any psychic or spiritual phenomena whatsoever. She told me she was going to mass to pray for me and was going to say the rosary. So I just let it be and put it down to an unusual experience.

The next morning much to my surprise I received a phone call from my mother, who was talking very fast. I couldn't understand what she was saying and had to tell her to slow down. She finally said, 'You know how you had that experience, well I just wanted to say it was the anniversary of your father's death yesterday,' and then she put the phone down. I smiled broadly to myself. I knew for sure that my father had come to see me and was comforting me. My father's love was unconditional and he made an extra effort to make his presence known to me.

Later on that same month I had another experience that was also very physical and special. As a single mum I did my best to survive and put the best effort in when it came to my working life but my confidence was very low. It was easy to let people get to me. I wasn't at all happy at work and had decided that the people didn't like me. I woke in the morning to hear my father saying, 'There is nothing wrong with you, people just take advantage of your good nature.' The message was loud and clear, giving me peace, comfort, healing and advice.

Over the years I have learnt the discipline of budgeting, and how to be a mother and father at the same time. Even though I had a very busy life and had good friends around me, inside I was lonely and feeling very much like I really wanted a special person to come into my life.

# *Good friends*

Good friends are always around you in important times in your life and I have many fun memories of Alice driving over to see me with a bottle of wine in her red Honda with a bent aerial. We would sit on my porch deep in conversation, drinking her wine and puffing away on cigarettes. I am pleased that I eventually let this unpleasant smoking habit go. I had taken it up as a way of calming myself through these tough times, but it was bad for my health and of course I couldn't afford it.

As well as Alice and Amanda, I made two new friends, a couple called Eleanor and Peter. Previously when my daughter had attended Star of the Sea Primary school in Howick, I attended a ceremony to open a new classroom block. I saw an amazing tall woman who looked so much fun. I could not believe she would be a Catholic mum and I decided I really wanted to meet this woman.

A few weeks later I attended a school meeting for mums interested in coaching or umpiring netball. There she was, sitting at the front of the classroom. Volunteers were asked to raise their hands to do umpiring so I raised my hand and Eleanor looked up and saw my hand raised and decided to join in. After the meeting we sat together in her Jeep and had an amazing conversation. Not long after this she invited me to a jet-skiing competition that her husband was hosting. They said they came from Inver Vegas — of course I thought they meant Las Vegas in the States — months later we all had a huge laugh about it, because they actually came from Invercargill.

This was a very busy time, working full time, bringing up three teenage children along with coaching and umpiring netball. On the other hand it also kept me busy. Peter, Eleanor's husband, was also very kind to me. They welcomed me into their home, family and hearts and to this day we are still all very good friends.

Unexpectedly around this time Todd had phoned me from the States and told me he still loved me. Although I was keeping busy I still felt very lonely. I knew I still had feelings for him, but he wasn't right for my children. He told me he would pay for me to come over and see him at Christmas time, and that he would pay for everything.

My family and friends were very supportive and agreed this was an amazing opportunity for me to get away from New Zealand and see the States. They agreed to look after the children for a couple of weeks, so off to America I went. About a week before I left I broke down in tears; I knew that Todd was not right for me but for some reason I had to go to the States, there was something important for me there.

For the first time my mother agreed to have Christmas dinner with me and the children. I knew at 4pm I would be leaving my home and be taking off for the airport. All was in hand with my children and after dinner they were off to stay with family and friends. Todd had given me very specific instructions about how to get on the right plane in Los Angeles to travel to Las Vegas where we planned to meet. Fortunately I had saved a small amount of money so I wasn't totally reliant on Todd all the time I was there.

After a 12-hour journey I arrived in Los Angeles with all the air hostesses wearing festive reindeer antlers. What a laugh! So, here I am Christmas morning in the States about to start a whole new Christmas day again. I had always thought that I didn't want Christmas day to end, but to be honest I was really over Christmas by that time. I eventually arrived in Las Vegas and headed down the elevator to meet Todd, who was holding a red rose in his hand. Something did not feel right at all. My heart sank. I just knew the connection was no longer there.

Regardless of this we spent the two weeks together, some of it in Vegas, Lake Tahoe, Santa Barbara and San Francisco. Something was amiss. When Todd's family phoned him, he didn't mention I was there, and when I met his friends he introduced me as one of his 'lady friends'. I was clearly nothing special to him at all.

However I had come to the States for another reason and that was to visit the Grand Canyon. It was one of the most incredible spiritual experiences I have ever had. There was something about the energy of the place, the atmosphere and the Indian music playing. I felt a strong energy and presence of spirit all around me. Over and over again I heard these words: 'You are special, you have a gift, we need you, the world needs you, and we need you to do this work full time. You were born to be a medium and this is your life's purpose.' I heard this message so clearly and it felt so right, I knew what they were saying to me was true.

I began to doubt whether it would be possible as I had three children to feed and keep a roof over their heads. Why on earth would spirit say this to me? It didn't make sense. I had worked part time doing readings, while working full time elsewhere, and this always helped to bring in extra funds when I needed it. I told myself to come back to my senses and let the whole experience go.

The trip to the States was full of magic, I had had a spiritual awakening inside and I knew that the spirit world had more in store for me. I knew that my spirit guides wanted me to work full time as a psychic medium, but I had no idea how this would unfold. I felt there was no choice but for me to put this worry aside for the time being as I knew and felt that what was given to me was real.

Often when we are given information which is potential or a prediction, we don't always understand how on earth this could occur in reality. If I see my clients are confused, I draw two marks on a piece of paper, one with a beginning and one with an end. I say, 'This is the prediction and potential that has been given to you. Right now at this present moment, you see your life as a straight line, black and white and you cannot understand how this could occur.' Then I draw two more lines with a beginning and an end and instead of the line in between being straight I draw squiggles to get to the other end of it. I say to them that life is more like this, it is never straight forward, just let go and allow the process to happen. This is exactly what I had to do with the information that was given to me in the States about my future. I knew it would happen and yet I had no idea about how or when.

My time with Todd had been fun, but he was obviously distracted. He left me feeling very empty and sad at the end of it all when he dropped me at the airport, turned his back on me and walked off. I arrived back in New Zealand feeling confused, sad and let down without much direction. My brother said to me, 'Kerry, you think you are heartbroken now, you have no idea how heartbroken you would have been if you had stayed with this guy.' He was so right.

Around this time Daniel made contact and wanted to see me again. Once again I was influenced by a well-meaning yet opinionated person who told me not to have anything to do with him. She composed a very hurtful email to Daniel and told me to send it to him and stood over me and insisted the email was sent. It was the same powerless feeling I experienced as a child. I went along with something that I knew was not right, I felt I had no choice, and I had to please someone else and do what they told me to do.

When I heard from Daniel later on, he could not believe my cruel words and no matter how much I explained it was not my idea he said to me, 'Kerry, I don't care. You still went along with it and sent the email.' I knew he was right. Sometimes saying sorry is just not enough. The damage is done. All you can do is ask for forgiveness, forgive yourself and move on. A psychic had warned me about watching what I said to Daniel but once again I was influenced by someone else, and hurt not only myself but a special person in the process. There was a big rift between Daniel and myself from that time onwards and the friendship started to weaken.

Later, there was a little healing in my relationship with Daniel which I believe was the work of spirit. I had a very vivid dream about his new relationship. The dream was about him and the lady he was with and I was told that his parents were also interfering with their relationship. I was told that he had to stand by her, that he was going to marry her and have a baby boy with her. I contacted Daniel about my dream and shared with him the warning I had been given. He was very surprised, and told me that his parents had been interfering in his current relationship. He thanked me so much for sharing my dream with him and said it was a very unselfish thing for me to pass this message onto him. Further down the track Daniel did marry his new lady and together they had a baby boy. I was so happy for him because I knew he would make such an awesome father. I accepted it was the right thing for us to go our separate ways, live our own lives and I was at peace with this.

I found a book called *Positive Gems* that Daniel had given to me years ago, and I started to read it every Friday at work and share lovely quotes with my work colleagues. These days I understand about the 'law of attraction' — without realising it, by becoming more positive in my outlook I was drawing new and better things into my world.

I felt a wee bit stuck and knew that I had to change the energy around me and make a shift in my life and so I decided it was time for a new job and a new home. I wanted to shift back to the North Shore. Whenever you feel stuck in life, it is always best to look at doing something new. This usually moves the energy. It does not need to be a major change. I met up with a real-estate agent who was very negative and told me quite bluntly that I had to either do up my house or stay where I was. I remember looking him in the eye thinking, 'Don't tell me to give up, you don't know how tenacious I am when I want something to happen.' Tenacity has often been my strength over the years. I knew that if this was meant to be, it would be.

Whenever we know we have to do something that it is right for us, things will start happening. Synchronicity occurs. I decided to employ Green Acres to mow my lawns in Howick and I had a lovely conversation with the female owner. I told her about my desire to shift to the Shore where my friends and family were based. She could see the problem straight away and told me to get some new curtains from Spotlight, and that for $1000 she and her team would clear my garden and scrub my house, totally spring clean the whole thing and get it ready to put on the market. She said that with a few new cushions and some flowers on the table, it would sell in no time. I am convinced that this was the spirit world looking after me once again as synchronicity started to kick in as it often does when you are on the right track.

I went ahead with the plan and swung into action sorting my

house out. I then met with another real estate agent, thankfully more positive than the previous one. We listed the house and put a large sign out the front of our driveway. I was in a quiet cul-de-sac so not many people would actually see the sign but I trusted all would work out for me.

My house had been on the market for only a very short period of time when one morning, I felt the urge to get something at the shops although I had no idea what. As I was backing out of my driveway I noticed an older couple slowly driving around the cul-de-sac looking at my For Sale sign. I thought, 'I am a sales person, I can do this,' and asked them if they would like to see my unit. They fell in love with it immediately. They did end up buying the property, and as the house had gone up in value I had enough for a deposit to start looking for a new property.

I was still hoping to meet someone special, and had started checking out internet dating. It was mostly quite hopeless, but it did give me many funny stories to share with my friends, and it prompted me to meet new people and get out of my comfort zone. I learnt a lot about what to do and what not to do online! After a while I decided that it really wasn't for me so gave it a long break.

I remember visiting some friends I knew from years gone by, who ended up living around the corner from me. This particular day I saw my friend's husband outside building a fence — he was quite a handyman and I can remember thinking, 'I just want a man like that, who is a handyman and can fix things.' It is true you very often attract what you ask for.

I took it as a sign when three different people on the same day suggested I join a site called 'Find Someone'. Amanda had also told me six months previously that the next man I was going to meet was called John. She reminded me that she had told me this once I had established my relationship with John further down the track, as I had completely forgotten, but I do remember saying at the time, 'That's my godfather's name.'

So here I was doing a wee bit of internet dating when a man called John approached me online. I told him I would not consider him unless he sent me a photo of himself and so he did. One thing that impressed me about him was that he had actually read my profile. He mentioned he liked the same book as me, *Who Moved my Cheese?*. He was a wee bit older than what I stated I was looking for, but he said he looked young for his age. I cheekily replied, 'Whatever!'

I was trying to find a property to buy on the North Shore, and Eleanor and my sister-in-law Priscilla were helping me. Eleanor was quite internet savvy and adored going on TradeMe, and before I knew it she had found the perfect house for me. Priscilla and I went to inspect this trendy townhouse in Bayview on the North Shore, and as soon as I walked in I just knew it was the one. I gave the vendor my offer immediately and we wrote it all down on a piece of paper. Priscilla was very impressed with my negotiation skills!

Even though Eleanor had kindly helped me find my new house, she was sad that I was leaving Howick. It was like the end of an era. Her husband Peter is an amazing cook and they invited the children and me to have the most fabulous meal with their whole family to say goodbye. It was a lovely occasion and I felt very honoured to be treated with such kindness.

# *Coming home*

My friends rallied around me with love and support as I packed up my life to head off to the North Shore. Alice had the job of picking up the keys from the lawyers and Amanda waited with me at the house to unpack. My new life was about to begin.

Around the time I shifted house I also decided to let smoking go completely as I knew it was affecting my health and energy. When you want to give up habits often a change of scene and routine can really help.

My middle son Andrew continued to rebel. He was a wee bit of a handful at the time and I was pleased when one of his friend's parents agreed to have him for a few weeks so we could have a much needed break from each other. At the same time my eldest son Benjamin decided to move back from university, and he brought his laptop and computer with him.

Synchronicity then really started to kick in. I awoke one morning to no hot water in the house. I had very little money after all the moving costs and was so worried about having to repair the hot-water cylinder. The neighbour came to my rescue. He looked at the hot-water cylinder and said all that had happened was the door on the cupboard had cut the wires. He re-wired it for me so

I had hot water back on in no time. Mum was very worried that my hot-water cylinder had been rewired by someone who wasn't an electrician and was convinced that I would not be covered by insurance in case of a fire. This is where fate was about to kick in.

I had been happy to give up on internet dating because I didn't have a computer at the time, but now that Benjamin had moved back home, that excuse didn't hold. A letter had arrived in the mail from a dating site that wanted me to pay my fees, so I had to go on the internet and sort it out. I was in the lounge with Cindy, Benjamin's girlfriend, and we decided to go onto Find Someone and have a giggle.

John, the man I had been cheeky to, had sent me a message saying 'Are you there?' I decided to answer him. After a while we started messaging each other but I never thought it would go anywhere. I thought he was bit cheeky when I told him I was going to a 70's-themed twenty-first party for my nephew and he asked me if I would be wearing hot pants!

It was a great party but I felt very alone when I saw all the happy couples together; there I was at a social function, the single one, yet again. Along with this I bumped into a couple who had been on the Catholic pre-marriage weekend with Daniel and me. The guy mentioned the pre-marriage weekend and said that the weekend had done its job because Daniel and I hadn't married. He said it with a grin on his face, like he was enjoying the pain I was suffering.

I became very upset, and phoned my friends Amanda and Alice. They both decided to come to the rescue. All at once I felt supported, and it made me realise how moral support in life's journey is so important. They laughed to see all the girls fluttering their eyelashes at my son Benjamin and then we all had a good laugh together. As a woman I have to say that life is so much better with girlfriends in it, for sure.

John and I decided to have a telephone date. We chatted for a while and he said he had his own electrical sub-contracting company, and that he was not in a rush to get into a serious relationship with anyone. I casually mentioned my hot-water cylinder and that my mother was very concerned that it had not been checked by an electrical inspector. John suggested if I needed some help with it to give him a call and he would send one of his guys out to take a look at it for me.

It was so nice that John offered his services, but I was determined that I would sort this out myself somehow. Mum kept insisting I get the cylinder checked, and would call me at work to remind me. After one particularly forceful call, I opened the White Pages and at the top of the right-hand page was *Callander Electrics* in bold print. I knew this was John's company so I decided to phone him.

Once again synchronicity was kicking in. Spirit was behind this whole thing, driving it forward. Even though we all have free will, I believe that there is always a bigger picture. A plan and opportunities are presented to us, however we have to be willing to take action for the plan to fall into place.

John answered the phone in a happy voice and listened as I sheepishly explained that I still needed my hot-water cylinder looked at. He responded, 'Not a problem, I will come and have a look at it for you on Saturday.'

After a quick shower and on with the makeup, I was ready to meet this new man John, who was coming to inspect my hot-water cylinder. Meanwhile, my car had been hit and my neighbour had come over to see if he could fix it. John arrived and I felt very natural and at ease with him. My daughter, Julia, joined us to suss out this man I had met on the internet. John inspected the hot-water cylinder and said all was well so I breathed a sigh of relief. I asked him if he would like a coffee — little did

I know he adored coffee — and so the jug was put on and the biscuits laid on a plate.

Julia instantly liked John as he seemed shy and unassuming. When he introduced himself he said, 'Hi, I'm John,' and looked down like he was a bit embarrassed. She started to interview John to make sure he was what he said he was. She wanted to know all about him!

I had friends coming over for dinner and I invited John to stay. He couldn't stay, but said he would come back and see me after dinner. He returned as promised and we talked until about 3am in the morning before I sent him on his merry way. We seemed to get on very well and he appeared to be a lot more real and genuine than any of the other men that I had met on the internet. There was a real honesty about him that I admired.

My mother continued to be there for me and had become my best friend. Even though we did not see eye to eye about our spiritual beliefs and I tended to hide my psychic ability away from her, I often asked her to pray for me when I was in sticky situations and her prayers seemed to always work. I knew at this point that religion tended to divide us, whereas working with spiritual energy unites and brings peace. I continued to work as a psychic medium off and on for quite a few years but I was a total closet medium over this time period, which meant that I did not develop further as a medium as most of my energy was spent on working, raising a family, dealing with the realities of life along with personal development.

Having my mother back in my life was healing, she was a real mother to me over this time and it was almost as if she was making up for lost time. I often feel that women in society are not always supported as mothers and that depression not only affects them, it affects their relationships and family as well. My mother was an amazing grandmother to all her grandchildren, and they all loved her dearly as did her daughters-in-law. It was like she took stock of herself and recovered from whatever she had been going through when I was in my formative years. At the same time she knew she had not been there for me fully when I was a child and she acknowledged this. Apart from that fact I was being a closet medium we started to have a more honest, loving and sincere relationship.

I witnessed other people in my life who carried bitterness towards their family or parents and I could see how this often drove them mad in the end and took away their sense of inner peace. It showed me how important it is to forgive. People do their best, they are not perfect but they are going through their own trials and tribulations. At the same time I had to forgive myself for the mistakes in my own life and my broken marriage and the hurt this had caused my children. Despite all of this I am truly grateful for my children's great courage and strength of character that seemed to pull them through life and is still with them.

After my first meeting with John I didn't hear from him for a while. I thought this was strange but I continued on with my life as usual. One afternoon I had just completed my weekend grocery shop at Pak 'n' Save and I had a sudden impulse to send John a cheeky text message. I had nothing to lose and if I didn't hear back from him then so be it. After I packed my groceries into my car I sent him a text 'Hello Mr long time no see'. Suddenly my phone was ringing and it was John on the other end asking how I was. We chatted for a while and he asked me out on a date to a guy at work's thirtieth birthday the following weekend. I agreed to go along with him.

The following Saturday I was all dressed up, waiting to be picked up by John, when I heard a loud motor of a V8 Ford arrive in my driveway. I looked out the window to see John in his new emerald car. I mentioned how flash his car was and he seemed very proud of his new purchase and the story behind why he bought it. We managed to get lost on the way to the party but got there in the end.

The evening went well and I enjoyed the company of his friends and work colleagues. I hoped I would see John again. I let him know not long after this that I was not interested in a casual relationship. I didn't want to come across as needy or desperate, however I wasn't interested in being mucked around and wanted to make my position clear.

He seemed a bit cagey at the beginning of our relationship and from the work I do now I often witness that men find it very hard to go through a divorce because of their children. John had been separated for nearly five years when I met him but had not legally divorced. I met his children on Guy Fawkes night and in my mind this is when our relationship really started, but I could see that John was not yet fully committed.

As a psychic I am extremely sensitive, which is a double-edged sword. Often I pick up on other people's energy very strongly, what is happening for them physically and emotionally. At the time I met John I could pick up the sadness his children were going through in relation to his separation and divorce, and I found it hard to deal with as I often felt the pain of their hurt and confusion. Early in our relationship, I had to establish with him that he was indeed positive he was doing the right thing by not going back to his marriage. I wanted to make sure of this before we could move forward.

Early the following year things started to pick up in our relationship, especially after a trip to Whangamata where I met John's brother and sister-in-law, who had been visiting from Ireland. We seemed to get on like a house on fire. John's son Dion and my daughter Julia also seemed to get on very well and we could hear them talking well into the night at an apartment we stayed at.

John reminded me one morning while we were in Whangamata about my comment that I was not interested in a casual relationship. He announced that morning that he really wanted to give things a go with me and see where it would lead. This is when we both fell in love.

Our romance started to blossom and we went through the ups and downs of a blended family scenario. I think one of the things that really helped both of us was doing a blended family course. It gave us a great understanding of what blended families are all about and how huge and complicated they can be compared to nuclear families. The course pointed out that each parent needed to spend time with their own children without the other partner being involved, so we both started to appreciate and respect each other around this. I had wished for these things in a man: someone who was a businessman, who had goals in life and was intelligent, someone I could love and have fun with and someone who was good at fixing things. My wishes had indeed come true as John possessed all these qualities. Talk about the 'law of attraction'!

Early in our relationship John informed me that he wasn't really into the psychic stuff and that was one of the things that put him off contacting me too much in the beginning. So I did a silly thing that I see a lot of woman do. I gave up what was a big part of me. I turned my back on my psychic and spiritual work to please my man.

# 23

## *Claiming who I am*

One weekend John went away for a boys' weekend and I started doing some thinking. 'What on earth am I doing?' I thought. I had given up my spiritual work for John and I was also allowing myself to be dragged along to watch heavy-metal bands that I really didn't like. I decided there and then that as much as I had fallen in love with this new man, it was time for me to be real, to be honest and actually ask myself why I was compromising something that was such a big part of me. I decided over this weekend that I was prepared to walk away from the relationship if I was not allowed to be me.

John arrived back smiling and happy from his weekend away. I announced to him not long after we had dinner together that I had decided to pursue my spiritual work again. I accepted him as he was and I understood that his music was a big part of him but at the same time my spiritual work was a big part of me. I told him very honestly that if he couldn't accept this was the real me then that was OK, but I wasn't giving it up for anyone. I expected some sort of reaction from John at this point but he simply looked at me and said 'OK' with a smile. At that point I could feel peace coming from deep within myself and I knew I had done the right thing.

For about 18 months there was lots of driving between each others' houses. We eventually decided that it was time to try moving in together and not long after that we shifted into a new house. At that time I was a sales manager for a medical publishing company. I thoroughly enjoyed my job and life had started to improve for me. I eventually sold my home on the North Shore, and instead of being in huge debt I ended up with quite a large sum of money that I invested later on in a house with John that would become our home. I was so thankful for the help and advice that Alice had given me over the years and realised the importance of managing your finances and the power of positive thinking.

During this time Amanda introduced me to a lovely young man called Adam who worked as a builder, who had the gift of what is known as trance mediumship. This is when the medium goes into a semi-conscious state and a guide or a collective of guides blends with their energy and they speak through them sharing philosophy, wisdom, joy and peace. Even though I had been involved with both psychic work and mediumship I did not know about trance mediums at this point. I saw Adam go into a trance where he told me that John would propose to me and that we would have a large wedding with all the bells and whistles, that we were soul mates and that his daughter would be having a child.

It all sort of blew me away at the time. I was not sure at all if John would propose as he said he was really not sure about getting married again and, even if he did, I could not imagine him wanting a big flash wedding. Also, his daughter was in her teens so a pregnancy was not likely at all. When we arrived home, Adam met John and told him his daughter was going to have a child and described the house she would be living in. Of course this was the last thing John wanted to hear.

Around this period we had friends that were very excited about a multi-level marketing business and wanted us to get involved with them. I was not that keen at first but somehow we got caught up in it all and so I ended up leaving my job as a Sales Manager to work for John part time selling electrical services and work on this new multi-level marketing business. When I started working for John I sold some advertising for my previous employer and saved enough money to put towards a family trip to Rarotonga that John's father was arranging for his eightieth birthday.

Off we went on an adventure to Rarotonga with all six kids, and not long after our arrival at the resort none of our six teenage children were to be seen. We eventually decided to take a walk to the beach and pop into the bar and there they were together drinking cocktails. Everyone seemed to be having a ball on the holiday and John's father enjoyed getting his surprise cake and the whole celebration. The next evening we were at John's brother's holiday place for dinner as they had flown over to Rarotonga too, all the way from Ireland. Someone that night seemed to have a bee in their bonnet about people in New Zealand getting married but never staying together. I was horrified to hear this and thought to myself, 'Be quiet, you are really going to put John off proposing to me one day.' I let it be known that I knew many people in New Zealand who had been married for many years and were very happy, and the subject was dropped.

That evening when I was looking up at the stars, John came up behind me and gave me a big hug. He said he wanted us to go back to the resort. He seemed to be in a particularly romantic mood so off to the resort we went. I thought he wanted to head back to our room but to my surprise he wanted to go to the bar for a drink. As we were walking along I stopped at a pergola and told him how romantic it was and how it would be a great place for someone to get married. He seemed a bit edgy and just wanted to get to the bar for a drink. He went away to get drinks when an older man approached me and started telling me a sad story of how he was alone and that his girlfriend wouldn't come with him on his holiday. I was chatting away when John came up to me looking a bit agitated and annoyed at the man taking up my time. He impatiently walked me off to sit outside with him and as soon as I sat down I spilt my drink everywhere.

We replaced the drink and he shuffled me away even further, where there was nobody around. As soon as we sat down John slapped his hands on his legs and said, 'Well I have decided that I want to spend the rest of my life with you Kerry, will you marry me?' I was in total shock and instead of replying 'yes', I looked out to the water and looked back and said, 'John, I can't believe that you are actually doing it!'

I kept thinking, 'I know that I want to marry John, but what about his kids, how will they feel?' Then I heard Elizabeth in my ear saying, 'It will create a stronger bond and in the end all the children will be happier as they'll know where they stand. You will be a unit, things will improve by you marrying.' I knew as I heard her soothing words that it was the right thing to do. I replied, 'Yes of course, I would love to marry you.' We had tentatively looked at engagement rings earlier and there was one I particularly liked but I didn't think John would actually go through with it! He produced the ring all ready for me to wear.

So the celebrations started and my children, along with John's father, sister, brother and family were happy. I could see that John's children needed some time to let it all sink in, and I respected this.

Our children seemed to be having a wonderful time and then unfortunately Andrew started to get sick and then John's son and daughter also fell ill. We ended up at the doctors and the Rarotonga hospital. The children all went back to New Zealand together as planned so John and I could have a final few days together. We finished off our time in Rarotonga with my mind ws spinning with excitement, already planning my wedding. The lonely times struggling on my own were over. I was about to enter into a new chapter in my life.

# A time of growth

John and I returned to New Zealand, excited about the future. John is an entrepreneur and a very clever man, one of the hardest-working men I had ever met. I have always admired how he started his electrical sub-contracting business from scratch. In many ways he reminded me of my father because of his intellect, hands-on ability, and the fact that people loved and respected him. My son wrote a paper about John for one of his university courses about the qualities of a typical entrepreneur personality.

When I started with Callander's I sold electrical services to hotels, business and fast-food chains. Along with this I kept plugging away at the multi-level marketing business, which I began to enjoy less and less. I decided to get some guidance from a psychic, who said there was lot more money to be made in John's business than in multi-level marketing. I agreed, but I didn't know how to tell John I wanted to focus on the electrical business. The business coach wrote down all the things I said and one of them was 'Sorry and I love you'. When I asked his advice about what do, he pointed to these words. With this phrase in mind I told John I didn't want to do the marketing business any more. 'Sorry and I love you'. John seemed to accept it well.

Being a salesperson had been a big part of my life so I soon decided to get more involved in the electrical business, chasing business and following up quotes.

I started setting up appointments, persuading John to go with me to meet with clients. They were happy to see us and business started to improve. I also saw other areas where we could improve the business, and we employed the services of a business coach which helped us greatly. I really enjoyed getting involved with the business.

Managing staff was a new skill for me. I don't know why but I thought it was best to be authoritative with the staff. The staff admired and respected John and we ended up in a 'good cop, bad cop' situation, with me as the bad cop.

I was acting like a powerful, assertive woman but this wasn't really me. I spent a lot of time in tears as the staff took exception to the changes I was making. Most psychics and mediums are sensitive people because they are working with their senses all the time. However my heart was in the right place and with everyone's hard work the company started to improve. I started to gain some respect from John's staff.

John could see I was struggling in my position so he enrolled me on a course on communication and change. I learnt that all humans have a basic fear of rejection and that we will not be loved or accepted. One of the hardest things people find is change.

Spirit must have been steering me to get me into a place where they wanted me to be. I think they wanted me to work for John because it was going to be easier and simpler to ease into something completely different, which was to work for spirit.

Adam's prediction came true and I started planning a rather large wedding. I don't know where the funds came from to pay for it all, as I paid for some things and John paid for others, but somehow we managed to get everything together for a large wedding. I became stressed about the whole thing and wanted everything to be perfect.

Over this time I became very confused about the Catholic faith. I just wanted Mum and my family's acceptance. It was a difficult situation because even though my marriage had been annulled a few years earlier, at the time John had been baptised an Anglican. His first marriage was a civil ceremony, and in order for us to marry in the Catholic Church he would have to get his previous marriage annulled. There was no way I would consider even asking him to do this. It would have been absurd.

I employed an Anglican Priest who had once been a priest in the Catholic Church to conduct the ceremony. Amanda helped me very much when she said to me, 'Kerry, you haven't been to church or had communion for years, and you are really into your spiritual work. Why are you still trying to hold on to the Catholic religion?'

When someone confronts you with the truth, things can become quite clear. When Amanda confronted me, suddenly the penny dropped and my confusion lifted. I realised she was right, a feeling of peace came over me and I let the illusion of a Catholic wedding go once and for all.

I was terrified my mother would be angry with me, as she had refused to go to one of my brother's weddings because he did not get married under the umbrella of the Catholic Church. To my surprise she was very accepting about the whole thing, just like when I told her I was moving in with John 18 months earlier. She had softened in her old age.

The wedding was a beautiful day. I was so thankful for an old friend who took care of me that day. The evening before she had laid my veil carefully across the bed along with beautiful towels with roses embossed on them that she had bought for us as a wedding present. Roses had become the theme of my wedding without me ever realising it.

Eleanor and my daughter Julia were my bridesmaids, and my niece was a flower girl. Amanda helped me with my dress and jewellery and Alice came along to the wedding to enjoy all the fun. My eldest son Benjamin gave me away, and he gave the most amazing speech. I was so happy that we had practised a special dance as my mother loved dancing. A darling friend offered to video the wedding and there is a special part where my mother walks forward to the special dance. Mum was very proud of the cake that she provided, which was rose-themed. I made sure there were six roses at its side, which represented our six children.

A few days later we flew off to Thailand for our honeymoon. We spent most of our time in Phuket, learning to barter at the markets, and also rode elephants and took a jet boat to an exotic island.

Six months later, I received a phone call from my mother with some bad news. We were very good friends by this time, and would chat on the phone nearly every day. This particular day she started off the conversation with, 'You are going to be angry at me.' She had a lump in her breast about the size of a golf ball, and needed to have a biopsy.

I was so grateful to be working for John as I knew he would be fine with me taking time to take my mother to the hospital. Unfortunately the news was not good and the lump proved to be an aggressive cancer, so Mum, aged 85, was booked in for a mastectomy. We also found out that John's daughter was pregnant, as Adam had predicted. She was in her late teens; I was so worried for her and did not know how she was going to cope. Mum said to me, 'Don't worry Kerry, babies always bring their love.'

I was so anxious while Mum was in surgery, and afterwards I wasn't allowed to see her as it wasn't visiting hours. The Charge Nurse saw me at the café looking upset, and remembered me from our nursing days back in Thames. She said, 'You were so kind to me back then, driving me back to Auckland every weekend so I could see my parents. Don't worry, I'm going to let you into the ward to be with you mother.' Isn't karma great?

Eventually Mum came to stay with us to recover from her surgery. I would shower her and look after her the best I could. However the news was not good. The cancer had spread into her lymph nodes and lungs. I was a complete mess, and remember Mum saying to me, 'You're really a good kid.'

As Mum's health deteriorated, she took turns staying with my brothers and their families. When her mind deteriorated, she came back to live with me. She seemed to be quite angry but I learnt that this was all part of the process.

My brother and his wife gave me a very good book called *Crossing the Creek*. It explains the dying process and what the dying person is going through. I realised that I was trying to keep my mother alive instead of accepting the process and helping her through it. Visitors came and went. It was particularly sad when Mum's best friend, Aunty Jennifer, came to visit She could not cope with the fact that her best friend was dying. One morning I caught Jennifer whispering in Mum's ear when my mother loudly proclaimed, 'Jennifer, you naughty girl! You'd better go straight away and see the priest.' My mind boggled as to what on earth darling Aunty Jennifer could possibly get up to at 82 years of age.

As sad as it was, the dying process is also interesting. I noticed huge changes in my mother. She started telling me about the spiritual experiences she had during her life. She told me about a monk, a Scottish man and a lady who would stand by her bed. They were very nice but she didn't like them being there, so she told them to go away because they weren't Jesus and she didn't trust them.

One evening she woke up and said, 'Number four is one of the most important numbers in the universe.' I told Amanda about this, and she explained that in sacred geometry the number four was the number of evolution and where we came from. Then my mother told me about a cat that kept hanging around. My English neighbour told me that her mum was a Catholic medium, and would talk about the 'ghost cat' that often protected souls who were going to heaven.

One night I couldn't sleep, so I got up at about 3am and went downstairs to make a cup of tea. As I looked around what did I see but a transparent cat. I nearly dropped my cup of tea!

John and I had started looking for a new home and we wanted to buy something either in Hobsonville or West Harbour, as I loved the Shore, he liked central Auckland and we both wanted a view of the water. Hobsonville was only 20 minutes from our work. When we found the home we are now living in it seemed far too expensive but there was just something about the home we found hard to resist. The couple who owned it were lovely and the lady was extremely spiritual. I could feel the amazing spiritual energy as I walked through the home.

My sisters-in-law were all very helpful with Mum. They would come and bed-bathe my mother or take over her care so I could have a break. We had just found our house and were on the way home when we had two very sad phone calls. One call was to tell us that John's daughter's best friend's mother had unexpectedly passed away. She was a lovely woman and I had often spent time chatting to her. I felt so sad for her daughter. Just a few seconds later I received a phone call from Priscilla to say that Mum was on her way out. It was all too much to take in, so we raced home. I knew I was not ready to let my mum go. We'd had a tiff in the morning and I could not stand the thought of her passing without us resolving things.

Everyone started arriving at the house to say their goodbyes. Our home was filled with her children, grandchildren, their partners and great-grandchildren. It was a house full of love and warmth. John was the best host ever as he made sure everyone was looked after.

Two of my sisters-in-law are registered nurses, and one gave Mum a small dose of liquid morphine as she had started chain stoking (more commonly known as 'the death rattle'). Andrew, my son, and Jade, another grandchild, were arriving the next day to see their grandmother, but it looked as though they would be too late. After receiving the wee drop of morphine Mum seemed to come back to life again, saying 'Not yet.' She then sat up and looked around the room, saying, 'Look at you all, you are a load of sooks.' It was the funniest thing, very much my mother!

Mum also kept telling us to get the 'damned cat' out of the room, but there wasn't a cat there. Amanda popped in for a visit, and politely pretended to shoo the cat out. Looking back maybe the ghost cat arrived to protect her spirit on the way to heaven.

Mum would get really frightened and want to hold onto me. She said she was being taught telepathic communication, and would say, 'I'm scared, I'm scared, I'm scared.' When I asked her what was happening, she whispered in my ear, 'It's spiritual.'

In the morning she seemed right as rain again. She told me that it was all too much for me and that I needed to get a nurse to look after her. In the morning after she had rested she often seemed pretty normal but by the evening she seemed quite crazy again. Thankfully both Jade and Andrew were able to see their grandmother and say their goodbyes. Andrew spent a lot of time in our house during the last week of my mother's life.

I was so thankful to the hospice nurses, as they were ever so special, and also to the nurses who were sent to bed-bathe my mum. Even though I was doing most of the nursing myself, looking after someone who is dying is a heavy load. We gave my mother a bell to ring when she needed me and even to this day John jokes with me about Mum ringing the bell and calling out 'Kerry, Kerry, Kerry.'

I would read to her every day the poem I had written for her eightieth birthday called 'The Lady with a Heart of Gold'.

The lady with a heart of gold
A woman of soul
The kindest one you have met
A woman of character
One you could never forget

She came into this life
With a heart full of love
And is always faithful
To our God above

A life full of colour
With so much to share
A heart always generous
Beyond all compare

Strong is her faith
As solid as a rock
Some would say
'A chip off the old block'

Friends she has many
Who all love her dearly
They turn to her
When their hearts are weary
Many late nights
She worked till late
Hanging out washing
And cleaning the plates

With a balance of love
Six children she did bear
Nurtured them all
But sometimes despaired

Her husband was loving
Faithful and strong
In his blue eyes
She could never do wrong

'Ed,' she would say
Just once a year
'It's Auckland Cup day
So let's get out our gear'
So off to the races
They would both go
Ed soon learnt
To 'go with the flow'.

Grandchildren she has many
They light up her day
They think she's awesome
In most every way

Grandma has told them
How the world made her grow
'Those American Soldiers
Put on a great show!'

Her spirit is young
And will never grow old
So let's charge our glasses
To her 'heart of gold'.

Kerry-Marie Callander

About a week after Mum had seen Jade and Andrew, I was taking care of her one morning and she kept saying to me, 'Light, light, the light.' I pointed to the light in the ceiling but she shook her head and said 'Golden light' and pointed to the corner of the room. You would have thought I would have known what she was referring to but I honestly could not understand.

Later on that day my mother's health really started to deteriorate. She wanted to go to the toilet and had become a bit of a dead weight so thankfully Julia could help me with this. Things became worse later on. Her right arm started to swell and she told me she needed urgent medical attention so I phoned the hospice in a panic. Her hand was swelling badly and her wedding ring was getting very tight around her finger. Luckily Andrew was there and he worked out if he cut her ring in two places with plyers it would come off more easily without piercing her. The hospice nurse explained to me that I should just sit with Mum and this was her time.

Our family was called and Mum started taking her final breaths. She was looking at the corner of the room where she had earlier talked about the golden light and when she passed this was where she was looking. We all started saying 'Our Father who Art in Heaven' and I am positive this helped my mother pass over more peacefully.

My mum went to the other side on 6 February 2009. Amanda came to see me a day or two after this and told me that my mother was a very strong spirit, and had told her about a brooch that she wanted to wear when she was buried please. I had no idea about this brooch but trusted it would become clear. We had a family meeting about her funeral and my brothers agreed that I should pick the clothes that she would wear, Amanda came with me to her house. I could not believe my eyes when I walked into her bedroom; the brooch was right there on her dressing table. I knew that Mum's spirit was all around us and in fact I could feel her for quite a long time after she passed away. Of course I read the poem 'The lady with a heart of gold' at her funeral.

I had strained my right arm and shoulder from lifting Mum, and it wasn't getting better. As I took myself off to get massages to help my arm, I kept hearing songs about 'a heart of gold' and songs about 'thank you for helping' and 'I will love you always'. I knew it was my mother communicating with me.

Not long after her passing, I was very upset about a personal situation. I asked Mum why this had to happen, and as I went outside I heard the song 'Life is a roller-coaster, you've just got to ride it. Don't fight it'. I had a sense of my mother looking back at the world and seeing how she worried herself sick over the years about all sorts of things, trying to control me with her religious views. I knew that she wished she had just gone with the flow and that is what she was telling me to do.

I also knew my mother was around when I heard the song 'How far is heaven?' Not long after I heard that song on the radio I had a dream that Mum told me she passed on the Friday and it took her until Sunday to arrive in heaven, and that she had an appointment to see God. She told me three things that happen when you get to heaven.

1. That you get there.
2. That the people you expect to be there aren't.
3. The people you didn't expect to be there are.

The following week when I was feeling very upset about Mum's passing, a friend suggested we visit her house. I didn't want to go because the last time I'd been there, everyone was dividing out her possessions, but the material things didn't mean anything. It really hit me when my mother passed over that we don't own anything. All the diamonds in the world are worth nothing when you pass over to the other world.

My friend was quite persuasive, so we did go to the house. Once in Mum's unit, we saw all the memorials Mum had kept of people who had passed before her. For some unknown reason we went into the spare room, and there was a catechism Bible. I could not believe my eyes. There sitting on the Bible was a note in Mum's handwriting that said:

Three things that happen when you get to heaven:
1. That you get there.
2. That the people you expect to be there aren't
3. The people you didn't expect to be there are.

I knew Mum was communicating with me in my dream because I had never seen that note before. Isn't the spirit world amazing?

Something else very strange occurred not long after my mother passed away. I went to get in my car and on the windscreen was a pair of baby shoes. I had no idea how they could have got there. I decided to visit Mum's grave and became very upset when I arrived. I had an overwhelming impulse to dig up the grave as my mum was in there and I had to get her out! I broke down in tears, sobbed and sobbed and realised that grief was a very strange thing. As I was about to leave the grave John phoned to tell me that his daughter had just given birth to a little girl. It felt like one door had just closed and another one had just opened. Were the shoes on the front of my car that morning a sign from Mum about the birth of Amber's baby?

Not long after this, my son broke up with his girlfriend, met a new lady and had a baby son whom we welcomed into the family. We used to have regular family dinners where I would invite all the children and their partners. I walked in from work to see my son feeding his new son and Amber feeding her baby. We all looked at each other and laughed. Here were my children feeding their children!

Blended families always have their challenges, but all our children loved being aunties and uncles to the new arrivals. My mother was right: babies do bring their love for sure.

After a client had been in hospital with heart problems, I decided it was time to take a trip to the doctor and get my shoulder and chest pains assessed as well. My doctor gave me a thorough check-up, and, while it turned out that my heart was just fine, it was something else that totally threw me into a panic. I had a pre-cancerous condition and needed emergency surgery.

When things fall apart, sometimes people whom we expect to be there for us are not able to be for some reason, but there is always someone to help us along the way. This time it was my daughter, Julia, who gave me the very special gift of her time and energy. She also said to me in her matter-of-fact way, 'Mum, I don't like telling you this but since you met John I have noticed you've got a bit frumpy in the way you dress. I think we should go shopping together for some new clothes.' I was taken aback when she said this because I loved to dress up but had hidden this deep within myself for a long time.

Julia and I went shopping, and I thoroughly enjoyed the whole experience. I was so happy to be doing something for myself which I had not done for such a long time. It was like this part of me had been put on hold, like a caterpillar who had gone into its chrysalis. Through the upset of losing my mother and not being well myself it enabled my daughter to awaken something inside me, which enabled me to break out of the chrysalis and emerge as a colourful butterfly once more.

As a child I hardly had any clothes to wear and in my first marriage we simply had no budget for clothes, we just had to survive. I had a short period with Daniel when I could spend a little more on my wardrobe and then for many years as a single mum, buying clothes or spending any money on me was out of the question as the children came first. It was wonderful to break free to be me and express myself fully.

It was a tough time. I was grieving my mum and there were other legal issues going on. I had the surgery, then haemorrhaged afterwards, so was rushed off to hospital again. John popped in to see me in hospital and said the house we had fallen in love with in Hobsonville was for sale again and that the vendors were willing to drop the price. We decided this opportunity was meant to be.

Before long we were shifting into this gorgeous home. I work from home, doing my readings and workshops. I had always wanted a sanctuary, and that is exactly what my spiritual room has become for me.

# 25

## *See where your guides take you*

The time felt right for me to begin to focus more seriously on my spiritual work. Amanda approached me about doing a show with another well-known medium, and wanted to know if I was interested. I wasn't sure if I was ready to go on stage, but decided to give it a go regardless.

Just before the show I was helping Amanda with a stand she held at one of the spiritual festivals. She asked me to hand out flyers for the upcoming show, and when I asked her where she wanted me to go, she turned to me and said, 'See where your guides take you.' I will never forget these words.

I was doing the rounds speaking to various people when I bumped into a lovely lady who did Shiatsu massage, and she told me that she also worked as a medium as well. We had quite a long talk and I told her I was one of the mediums appearing in Amanda's show. I had butterflies in my stomach as I'd never done a demonstration and I was throwing myself in at the deep end.

This lovely lady then told me about the Arthur Findlay College in Stansted, England. My ears pricked up when she said she was going over there with a group of people in August. I somehow knew I would be visiting this renowned college at some stage, although I had no idea how I could afford to get there.

Not long before the show, I was in the shower one morning and I felt spirit come in strongly around me. I saw a flash of golden light and heard an eagle and thought, 'Oh my goodness, who is Golden Eagle?' I phoned Amanda, who was amazed when I told her my experience and said to me, 'That is Golden Eagle. He comes to all the teachers and is a very important guide.'

The medium who was going to do the show with me wanted to see me perform, so I did my first platform demonstration at the Silverdale Church. As I was about to start, I heard John arrive on his Harley Davidson motorbike and the whole audience broke into laughter. I became very aware of a male guide with me, and later on discovered this was my gatekeeper, Francis. I was so nervous during that evening and had no idea what I was doing but I persevered. The other medium was satisfied and said that I would be OK to work with.

Amanda and I visited the venue before the show, and took a photo of it. Later on when she brought the picture up on the computer screen, we both saw a golden heart appear on the image. When I kept looking at the photo I could see both my mother and father's figures and my father was behind my mum holding her. There was also another figure in the photo and on the right I could see a very large profile of a spirit guide, but I could tell he had a moustache. The guide's face was huge and the figures in the photo much smaller by comparison. It was amazing.

Amanda put on her show and I managed to talk my children into coming along with their partners. I was networking at a Business Networking International meeting at the time and somehow seemed to talk quite a few of the ladies from the group to attend as well. I think I brought through about three or four links, then handed over to the more experienced medium. My heart was pounding the whole time and I wasn't sure if I wanted to do that again. All the ladies who attended BNI were very positive people and they sent me emails saying how proud they were of me and how much they enjoyed the show. There is nothing like positive encouragement to push you forward in life.

Not long after the show I decided to really start working again as a psychic medium. I knew I was rusty however. I felt I really needed to get on the bike and start pedalling again, to work on improving myself and my gifts. I was learning to trust myself a bit more, and that was the day I met the lovely lady who told me about the spiritual college in the England.

We hadn't quite moved into our new house at this time so I had to find a place to work from. One afternoon I visited Goodey's bookshop, and the owner said I was welcome to rent one of her rooms there. I walked in full of confidence to meet a friendly lady behind the counter who introduced herself to me as Kara. I had a strong sense about this woman and felt she would be in my life. I said to her, 'I feel that we will be friends' and asked her if I could look at the room I would be reading from. I came with a handful of business cards and asked if she would give these to people and recommend me, she turned around and said very clearly, 'No I won't recommend you until I see how good you are. Why don't you come over to my house for morning tea and do a reading for me and my sister and then I will decide if I will recommend you. I am more than happy to pay for your reading'. John said to me later that it was fair enough that she had asked me to do this.

I met Kara and her sister the following weekend and they put on a yummy morning tea for me. I then started giving the reading for Kara and she was pretty blown away. Her best friend, Rhonda, came through and described herself perfectly, and even told Kara about how on her wedding day she had gone to visit Rhonda in hospital and had given her wedding bouquet to her. Other family members came in as well, and I certainly won Kara over that day. I had just decided to be myself and see where it went, and obviously the spirit world wanted us to be friends. Like Amanda, Alice and Eleanor, Kara would play a big part in my life.

I was correct in my prediction and we did indeed become friends. We often would spend time together and I would bring through spirit after spirit for her. It was like Kara was my practice ground for what I was going to do. She motivated me and gave me confidence.

About this time I got a reading from a very good medium and she confirmed that I had a male guide around me, a monk. If you ask spirit direct questions they very often don't answer you, but reply in a more cryptic way when you are relaxed. The answer is often very good but never quite what you expect. For example, if you want to know a guide's name they may never give it to you and if they do, it won't be delivered in the way you expect. I had been asking this monk's name, and was lying down on my bed resting with my daughter. I then noticed 'France' on a dream chart I had made, and I knew my guide's name was Francis. When someone asked me who my gatekeeper was, I had a strong sense it was Francis. I did a mediation and saw a monkey face and now whenever I connect to him he often shows himself as a monkey face. 'Monk key' means the monk with the key.

Ever since I was a child I had seen, felt and heard spirit, but I was very confused as I had been taught it was evil. I continually doubted myself. John and I had been invited to his aunt's eightieth birthday, so we flew to Wellington to stay with his father first and then drove up to Hawera and back after the event. On the plane on the way to Wellington, I put to the spirit world that 'if what I am experiencing is true and there really is life after death,

I want to see a dragonfly in three days.' I then completely forgot my request.

We drove up to Hawera and John's cousin invited us to stay the night. In the morning as I was making our bed, I felt hands touching me and turning me around. There was nobody there but when I looked ahead, there was a dragonfly engraved into the vase. I was speechless. I couldn't wait to tell John about my experience.

My husband loves coffee and on the way back down to Wellington he decided to stop for a coffee break. As soon as he saw a coffee sign he pulled over, and to my amazement when I looked up I saw a gift shop with a display of large dragonflies outside.

On investigating further, we discovered the shop was adorned with so many dragonflies it was unbelievable. I was determined not to buy one and thought, 'OK I have got the message!' As I left the shop and went around the corner, the shop owner called me back and showed me a dragonfly piece, how it could balance on my finger, then he put it in my hand and said, 'You can have it.' I was speechless. Spirit wanted me to have absolute proof of their existence without any doubt or confusion.

There are many meanings or interpretations regarding signs that we see. We can find different explanation for these signs. I believe spirit were having fun with me this day. Later on I was moved to google the meaning of a dragonfly and discovered that many cultures interpret dragonflies as 'the physical manifestation of life after death'.

## *Breaking free*

John and I were planning a trip to the UK so he could see his family in Ireland, and I decided to do a course and visit the Arthur Findlay College while we were there. I had absolutely no idea what I was letting myself in for.

John's friend drove me to the entrance of the College in Stansted. I could feel my heart beating, I was so nervous. John and his friend both came in with me and we headed to the second floor where I would be staying for the next week. There were photos of what I thought were ghosts on the museum windows. I felt quite frightened, yet John's friend seemed to be fascinated.

The wind coming through the open window was blowing the curtain around as we walked into my room. I said to John, 'That's it, I'm so scared. I don't want to be here, please take me back.' I was like a frightened child attending school for the first time. John's friend seemed to know exactly what to say, telling me, 'Don't worry Kerry, here's my phone number if you really can't stand it. Please phone me and I'll come and pick you up.' This gave me some comfort as I was really petrified by this stage.

I made my way down to the tea room and saw lots of people gathering there. Everyone was saying what an amazing energy the place had, but all I could think was 'Really? I'm sure this place is haunted,' as I helped myself to a cup of hot tea, trembling with fear. I met a lovely lady in the bathroom who also seemed very upset about saying goodbye to her family, and I was relieved to see I was not the only person feeling unsettled.

I started to get to know the other people over dinner, and slowly but surely I started to settle in a bit more. I remember looking at the lady opposite me — I was so taken with her eyes, there was something just incredible about them. They were almost angelic, and the love emanating from her was beautiful. Later on in the week this lady did a talk about how she'd had two near-death experiences, and how the guides had healed her and sent her back to her body on the earth plane. I also met another lady at the college who had the same look in her eyes, and she also spoke about having a near-death experience and how she had returned to her body as it was not her time. They both mentioned 'them and they and how they healed them'. There is something incredibly special about people who have had near-death experiences; their eyes have a certain amazing look about them.

We started our classes, and I was very happy with the tutor I had been allocated as part of our group. I just knew she was a very good teacher, and would know how to handle my nervousness. On the second evening we went to a Divine Service in a chapel-like room at the college called 'the Sanctuary' and I had never seen anything like it in my life. When the mediums demonstrated mediumship, it was out of this world. The evidence was unbelievable and any doubt I had about life after death was dissipated once and for all.

A most amazing medium demonstrated, and immediately I was taken by the dragonfly she was wearing around her neck. She talked about the spirit blending with her, gave the spirit's name, the names of her siblings, her address, their addresses, and lots of other very specific details. Another medium told a lady in the audience she had her sister in spirit; her sister had seen her shopping for a white pair of shoes which were on sale, and that the shoes didn't quite fit her so she'd taken them back for a refund. The lady who received this message just gasped as this event had only just occurred. The medium also went on to accurately say that they owned a budgie, gave the budgie's name, and described how it would come out of the cage to nibble crumbs from her lips.

After witnessing these demonstrations, I went from believing to totally knowing that the spirit world existed. I just wanted to learn and grow as a medium so I could bring evidence through of life after life, and bring through uplifting energy and healing to the bereaved.

I then went to see my tutor for a reading, which was fantastic as well. She called me Kerry, not Kerry-Marie. When I told her may name was Kerry-Marie, she shook her head and said, 'No, when you were born your first name was Kerry. Marie is your second name and you were called Kerry for most of your life.' I had to agree she was right. She told me how I was an outsider in my family and I replied, 'Yes, because I have five brothers and I am the only girl.' She shook her head again and said, 'No, you are separate and different from your family.' She then went on to say to me, 'Spirit are showing me that you are a beautiful butterfly and you have been pinned down your whole life, and now they are taking the pin out and setting you free.' I sat there with my mouth wide open. She was so right, I couldn't believe it. She also told me that I would be a platform medium and that I would keep developing more and more.

I had another very memorable experience with another student as we were working with symbols. She gave me an acting mask and straight away I knew she was referring to Daniel who had been a part-time actor. She then said, 'Your father is here. He is telling me you went to Italy with the actor. He is also telling me that you were very upset at the time because he had passed over and had not travelled much. He is telling you that there was no need to fret because he was with you the whole time, travelling alongside you, seeing everything you saw.' I nearly fell off my chair.

When it came time for me to stand up in front of the class and present my mediumship, I was shaking like a leaf and my tutor said, 'Kerry, what are we going to do about your nerves?' I took a deep breath and described an English man who felt like a grandfather, wearing a cap sitting outside a UK pub. The tutor asked everyone to stand up and as the evidence was given people had to sit down if it didn't apply to them. The tutor wrote the evidence I was given on a clipboard. I was positive I was imagining all of this when a young man at the front smiled back at me and said, 'That is my grandfather and I can take everything you have just said.'

Even though I had previously done a show and a platform demonstration in New Zealand and lots of private sittings, it is always a challenge getting up in front of a group of classmates who are also training mediums. I had to trust spirit and the information I had been given.

Early during the week at the college, I made friends with the lovely lady that I met on the first day in the bathroom as well as some of the others. We became very close in a short time. Often people who travel to the college from overseas come with someone they know and spend most of their time with that person. However, I've learnt that the advantage of going by myself is that very often I meet new people and become friends with people from all over the world.

The last night at the Arthur Findlay College was very emotional for everyone. We held hands as tears flowed from our eyes. No one wanted this amazing experience to end. Little did we know that we would all be together again the following year.

The week was just so special and I felt I had so much more to learn about mediumship. The college was a catalyst to push me forward. Mediumship is not something you can learn — you can only develop it by working with it. I worried that because I'd been to the Arthur Findlay College, people may expect me to have transformed into an incredible medium. In fact, I felt a lot more humble and aware of how I would always be developing and learning as the years went by.

I made some very significant friends on that first trip and our group didn't want to say goodbye to each other. I was impressed that these friends all had websites to promote their business, so I decided to do the same.

On my return to New Zealand, my son's friend kindly built a website for me without too much expense. Fortunately one of the girls I had met at AFC was an artist and did the artwork for me. I was terrified to come out in the open about my mediumship because I didn't want to offend my family, and there was no way that I was going to put my photo on the website. My friend Kara kept encouraging me, and reasoned that people might not trust me if I didn't include a photo. A life coach I was seeing at the time said, 'What's the worst thing that could happen with your family?' I was convinced that I would be kicked out of my family for doing this work as I had already experienced being shunned from the family a few years before when my marriage broke up.

About the time my mother was passing I was led to see a gentleman who was a very good counsellor. He was quite religious and was a Minister for the Salvation Army but he seemed to see the love in my eyes when I spoke about my spiritual work. We both agreed we believed in God and I knew I had met Jesus when I was 28, so I had no doubt about this at all. As I poured my heart out to him he said to me, 'Every time you speak about your spiritual work your whole face lights up. It gives you peace, it gives you security, it provides an income. This is what you are born to do'. I started to talk about what my family thought and he stopped me in my tracks, saying, 'You have tried to please others your whole life and it has not worked. All that really matters in life is what you think of yourself and what God thinks about you. It really does not matter what anyone else thinks.' It was like he was handing me the key to unlock the controls put on my life.

About this time my nephew contacted me to offer support. I told him about my website and how upset I was that one of my brothers had said at a business function, 'What is the silly bitch up to this time?' My nephew, who was no longer a child, replied, 'Aunty Kerry, nobody is kicking you out of this family again. Nobody'. Suddenly I realised things had changed and that I had the support not only of spirit but of some of the next generation in my family.

With Kara's encouragement, I launched my website. I decided to take her advice and put my photo up on the page. I initially called my website kerrymarie.co.nz and then felt moved to give it a name that was not mine. I heard spirit say to me 'Spiritual Decisions' and after a search to make sure nobody else was using this name, I was able to secure it for myself. I came out of the closet as a medium once and for all.

I went to the UK many more times to learn more and more, and kept growing as a medium. I was overjoyed with the evidence that kept coming through from spirit world. They would give me their names at times, what they passed with, a lot about their life, and shared memories that only the sitter knew about.

Even to this day when spirit comes through and gives me evidence, I am continually blown away with the amount of information and detail provided. I became very close to Kara over this time and we would spend a lot of time together discussing spiritual matters. It was like spirit was putting us together so she could encourage me through this time. I would bring through a spirit and sometimes she would know who they were and other times she wouldn't, so she would ask her parents and they would confirm exactly which loved one had come through. In total I brought through about 50 relatives and the information and evidence given was correct.

There was one reading that stood out, and it taught me a lot. I started off seeing a soccer ball and this lovely lady came through who used to smoke. Kara knew straight away that she was her children's grandmother, and she gave her some very good advice. Then I felt the energy of an older gentleman, who told me the most peculiar message. I heard him say so clearly, 'The lawn-mowing man was crazy!' Immediately I thought that I couldn't give such a ridiculous message. Kara heard me say, 'I can't give that message,' then he said it again. 'The lawn-mowing man was crazy.'

Kara finally said, 'Kerry-Marie, don't worry just give it,' so I repeated the message. She immediately said, 'Oh yes, I know exactly what he is referring to.' This gave me the confidence to give more information. I then saw a legal document and it had a stamp on it like someone had won a legal case.

Kara gasped when I said that, and said, 'Kerry-Marie, I don't think you realise just how amazing this all is.' She explained that the man who used to mow her grandfather's lawns had contested his will when her grandfather passed over. Of course he didn't win the case; the judge found in favour of Kara's family, hence the stamped legal document. Everyone thought he was crazy to think he could do such a thing.

This incident taught me to just give what I get given; don't try and make sense of it because even though it may not make any sense to me, it is likely to make sense to the sitter. It is about trust, letting go and keeping me out of it.

Interestingly, after my first trip to the UK I went to another tutor in Auckland who told me I would be teaching others very soon and in fact a lot sooner than I thought. I remember thinking, 'No way would that happen, I'm not ready.' However within a few months I was putting together my first teaching workshop.

John wanted to support me so he joined in the first day of the workshop and gave it his best shot. It all seemed to go very well and I got quite a buzz out of it. It was amazing seeing the students all start to develop as the day progressed. I had discovered a huge passion for teaching mediumship and spiritual work.

John gave me some very constructive feedback when he said, 'Kes, yes it was pretty good, but man you packed a lot of information into one day.' His feedback made sense, and from that point on I decided that keeping it simple was a lot better than having an information overload. I started to notice that the students enjoyed the workshops a lot more. Sometimes when I did a meditation I would see a wolf in my mind's eye; one of my friends from the spiritual college told me that seeing the wolf is a sign that you are a teacher. My passion for teaching others was confirmed yet again.

I kept in touch with the friends I met in the UK and before long we were planning a reunion only seven months later. My son and his young family had moved to London, so I had an excellent excuse for another visit to the UK. So off I went on the plane again, so excited to see my family and friends, and to go the Arthur Findlay College again.

This time round, I felt so much more comfortable and confident in my skin. It was such a joy to see my friends, and our time together was just as magical as the first time we met.

On my return from the UK I had a very emotional experience,

which has been one of my biggest lessons yet. Even though I do believe that when mediums are together they can link into the same spirit, I learnt that in this particular situation you can only go with the information you are getting and it is best to never listen to anyone else. I had a dream one night that a little boy had gone missing in Napier and that he had drowned in the water and his parents could not find him. A few months later my hairdresser told me about a little boy who had gone missing, and I knew this was related to the dream I had earlier. When John came home I told him I was going to phone the police because I felt I had information that would help them find the missing boy. He looked at me and warned, 'OK, but don't tell anyone that you are doing this, Kerry.'

John was so right. I so wish I had listened to his advice. I ended up confiding in some people who completely mixed up the whole thing for me.

When I phoned the police they were very helpful and were interested in listening to what I had to tell them. Without realizing it, I described the place he had last been seen and it was his favourite place to play and they also seemed to know about a younger boy that had been around him at times. I also said I felt he had fallen into a stream and he would be found 500 metres upstream and he would be found nine days later.

This is where I became confused. I had spoken to other people and I had information passed onto me from other mediums that he was trapped in someone's house. Someone else told me he was in Hastings in a barn. I felt obliged to give the extra information to the police. All I wanted to do was to help find the little boy but I knew deep inside that he was where I first had told the police, and they would find him in nine days from the time he went missing. The information that other mediums gave me at the time was completely incorrect, even though they believed they were helping me of course.

Then it was on the news they found the little boy nine days later and was found 500 metres upstream. I felt heartbroken for the loss of the little boy, for his parents and family. I had let them all down by getting so confused by everyone else's information and realised how right John had been when he warned me not to tell anyone about the fact I was contacting the police. He often said to me 'Loose lips sink ships.' This was one of my biggest lessons as a medium, to go with what I knew to be correct and not to get influenced by others.

A few months after this I had a dream that I was an Indian lady, I had a little daughter, I lived in Tauranga, I was terrified of my husband's brother who lived close by and I was petrified for my life and my daughter's life. In my dream I was begging my husband to move from the house but he would not listen. I could see evil eyes staring at me, I was inside this house and I could describe the whole thing in detail. I told John and a couple of friends about this dream and then three months later it was reported that an Indian lady and her daughter had been murdered by her husband's brother in Tauranga. I had been psychically tuning into her fear at the time. She was crying out for help.

I decided I was quite interested in psychic detective work and started training with a lady in the United States. Using a photo on the website, we had to tune in to whether someone was dead or alive. We were asked to give various details about the person in the photo, for example if they were dead, how were they killed, could we describe the weapon used, what did the murderer look like and so on. John told me it was like living with the Addams family. Even though it is very helpful to the families of missing people, it is quite dark work in a way and I noticed my skin started to dry out. It was like the nature of this work was affecting me physically.

At first I struggled with psychic detective work, but after a while I began to get it frighteningly correct. I can clearly remember that I started to see a crystal-clear image of a murderer, their weapon and where the murder occurred. It was at this point I thought, 'I'm going to give this up, it's getting all too real and freaky.'

The psychic detective training helped me to decide that it was important that I stick to my passion of mediumship and further develop in that area. Even though as a medium I often work with people in a state of grief, there can be a lot of joy in mediumship too, and it's a lot less sinister than the psychic detective work. Working with spirit to help people in grief find peace and comfort is what I want to do.

I used to do a lot of meditations around this time. I would email Kara about the information I received from people who were well-known in their time. The information would mean nothing to me, but Kara would do some research and tell me that the information I was given was indeed correct. It was so wonderful to have this confirmed, knowing that the information was spot on.

Through my meditation I was contacting higher and higher beings. While I was in meditation a spirit might walk through. It felt like my vibration had dropped and the vibration and energy of the spirit felt lower than that of the higher beings. I remember one time in my room when I was in meditation I was aware of an enormous, glorious angel. It felt like this golden angel was much larger than the room but still in the room, and the feelings of peace, love and comfort that emanated from this beautiful angel were immense. It's hard to put it into words, but it was truly glorious, something I will never forget.

Once when Amanda visited me, we decided to do a healing on her. At this stage I was not a Reiki Master like I am now and it was like I was being instructed by spirit how to perform a healing. Amanda is quite a powerful medium herself; I had no idea what an amazing thing was about to occur. Not long into the healing, while I was around her solar plexus area, she called out, 'What on earth are you up to? I can really feel that.' I looked down to see a foggy smoke-type substance all around her, which followed my hand wherever it went. The room was dim, with only a candle burning. The smoky substance was about 30 cm from her body and very, very real. I got terribly excited about the whole thing as did Amanda, as she opened her eyes and could see it as well.

I notice when I am doing a healing and the lights are off sometimes a smoky substance comes off my hands, particularly when I am working on the chakras. I have since learnt about physical phenomena and I am not really sure what this experience is, but I know it is from spirit and it is powerful.

One evening when I was dreaming, I was shown my hands reaching up, with lightning bolts coming off each finger. The bolts were colours of the rainbow. The next day when I was healing a lady I was thanking spirit and saying to them, 'I know this is coming from you and it has nothing to do with me.' I heard a voice as clear as a bell, 'We are a team.' I was being told that I needed spirit and they needed me as well to do healing work.

Kara phoned me one night to tell me about some health issues and that she needed some surgery to remove a mass. Of course I started doing a healing on her; she said she could almost feel someone touching her and doing something as I was doing the healing. Later on she told me she had been wiped out for a whole week after the healing session. We decided that maybe the healing had done something amazing, so I gave her a follow-up healing the next week prior to her surgery. She had the same experience as in her first healing session with me. After her surgery I went to visit her and Kara said to me, 'The surgeon is very embarrassed; he's done the surgery but there were no masses to be found and he cannot explain it.'

About a year later I was asked to do some healing on a lady who had a high-grade melanoma. Understandably she was very afraid. I was told to be very gentle and mindful with her in regards to her healing. I did two or three healings for her and to our amazement the grade lowered to a point where it was no longer dangerous, and the melanoma was removed safely and easily.

The power of spirit always amazes me. Healing is another form of mediumship where spirit can do their incredible work to help those in need. Of course when someone is going to pass over there is nothing you can do to stop this process, although it is always good to be open to the possibility of a miracle.

Along my journey I met another lovely spiritual young lady who had a very good gift of mediumship. One evening we had dinner together at her house, and then watched 'Sensing Murder'. Something very strange occurred. I had a phone call from my sister-in-law informing me that one of my cousins had just passed over and suddenly I felt like I was covered in cobwebs. I told my friend about this and I think she thought it was amusing.

As I drove home the cobweb sensation got stronger and stronger, and by the time I arrived home it was very intense. I opened my front door feeling as if insects were crawling over me. It was uncomfortable and strange, but not frightening. Intuitively I felt it had something to do with my cousin's passing but I couldn't quite work it out. I shouted out his name a few times and asked him to leave me alone, and that he needed to go over to the other world. The feeling left me. I don't know what had occurred but it was real. Sometimes phenomena is something you experience but cannot accurately describe.

Usually when I am doing spirit work or when I am meditating I feel a cobweb-type feeling, but never to the same intensity as on that particular evening. Often I will feel a tickling feeling around my head and sometimes I feel a spiralling feeling going into my crown chakra. It is a beautiful feeling, very comforting and I know that spirit is right there with me. Once I was meditating when I felt a finger touch my finger and for some reason it felt like my mother's finger touching me.

When doing readings I can often see flashes of light, sometimes bright white and other times gold. I know this is spirit confirming something with me. Sometimes I see blue or purple sparks, and I will say to my sitter 'Did you see that?' They never do but they often feel comforted and happy that I have witnessed it around them or in the reading.

My husband has become used to me over the years, when I wake up in the middle of the night saying, 'Can you feel the angels, John?' He tells me that sometimes he can feel something. Sometimes in the early hours of the morning I see swirly lights when I sleep, accompanied by an incredible feeling and soothing noise like a light ringing sound. It is very hard to articulate the feeling but it often feels like a visitation from a higher source. On my first visit to Arthur Findlay College my tutor was giving me a spiritual assessment when she stopped and said to me, 'They are telling me that you often get an angelic visit in the middle of the night.' I smiled as I knew exactly what she meant.

After my first trip to the AFC I went back on many occasions. I couldn't get enough of the place. On one of my visits I met a very interesting young man, who advised me that I would need to start taking some time off from my husband's work. He said it was going to get too much for me working full time and doing my spiritual work. He gave me some information about training formally under the Spiritualist National Union, which felt very confusing at first. Fortunately I met some other students at the college who were also doing this training, and started to learn more about it all. I had no idea I could actually qualify under the SNU (Spiritualist National Union), which is a recognised religion in the United Kingdom. I decided to pursue this path as it was the right time for me to do more formal training than I had being doing up until this point.

On the same trip I was learning more and more about meditation, such as how to quieten the mind. Our minds are very powerful and can be extremely busy. In one session I was in the well-known library at the Arthur Findlay College, and we were being taken into a deep meditative state. Out of the blue staring back at me was a Japanese lady dressed in a red kimono, and not long after that I saw a bearded Egyptian man wearing white garments with a veil and a gold band around his head.

Even though I don't have an artistic bone in my body, I was starting to get interested in psychic art. After the meditation I had a spiritual assessment booked with a very good medium and tutor, and not long into the assessment/reading she told me that I had a Japanese lady who was a guide dressed in red, and that she was going to help me with my new interest in psychic art. She also said that there was an Egyptian man wearing white clothing with a gold band around his head. I found it hard to believe that she described the two spirit guides I had just seen.

One thing I am very big on with both psychic and mediumship work is that there needs to be evidence. Without any evidence anyone can tell you anything and it can be dangerous and misleading. Hearing the evidence from my tutor was amazing and lead me to take an interest in psychic art.

After the course I met up with John in the UK, and we flew over to France. We visited a shop that I adore, which has very colourful clothes. There on one of the dresses was the Japanese lady looking back at me, so of course I had no choice but to buy this beautiful dress. That evening I had the most incredible dream: I was about to demonstrate mediumship, and a lady next to me told me she was a guide. She was in a wheelchair and mentioned the name Mavis Pittilla to me. The lady showed me how to demonstrate, and said that it was not a hard thing to do and not to worry, she would be next to me helping me. There were other things she gave me in the dream, including warning me about someone who had been in my life.

Approximately two years later when I was back at the college, we were being taught how to be in circles. An elderly lady told us that she felt Judith Fry was with us and that she was in her wheelchair, and that she was encouraging us all. Of course my ears picked up. I had to wonder if this was the lady from my dream two years earlier. After the circle I asked the tutor who Judith Fry was, as I'd a dream about a lady in a wheelchair and it sounded like her. The tutor turned to me and said, 'Mavis Pittilla's sister.' I gasped when I heard this, as it confirmed to me that it must have been Judith Fry who had visited me in my dream and who wanted to help me. What an honour!

Even though John is not really into spiritualism, he has always supported me in my work. I did a healing on him once, and saw a lady standing beside me wearing a maroon and gold veil. She told me that she was his mother in a past life, and that I was being too powerful with my healing and to calm down a bit. After the healing John was pretty non-committal and then out of the blue he told me that he had seen a lady above him during the healing, wearing a maroon and gold veil. He was trying really hard to get to her but he couldn't.

At one point during another healing, I became aware of a guide around John. The guide felt like a businessman, and he told me his name was George. In my first workshop when I was teaching the class meditation, John had mentioned that he had seen a man in a top hat, and I'd told him that this must be his guide George.

The interesting thing with John is that even though he is

not into the spiritual stuff, when it comes to past lives, he has expressed that he thinks maybe they do exist. There was another instance I was doing a healing for him, during which I had a vision of him being in a war. He was a solider and was killed. I described the specific colour of the uniform he was wearing and the white mud he had been walking in. Later on John said that it sounded like the American Civil War. On another occasion when doing his healing, I heard John's guide speak to me. He confirmed he was John's guide and told me his name was George Carmichael. He was helping John in business and he had been a banker in the American Civil War. We googled this later and there he was: George Carmichael, a banker in the American Civil War.

To me it is so important in my work that there is evidence. Evidence makes things very real and is comforting for the people I am helping. It's exciting to know there is life after life because the person we think we may have lost comes alive, even though it is in a different form to what we have known. Nevertheless having evidence of life after our physical life here on Earth gives us hope, knowing we will see our loved ones again. It gives a deeper meaning to our own life and what it is all about. Along with this comes peace to the mind, body and soul. A psychic or a medium can tell you anything, however unless there is some form of evidence given in the information, then personally I question it. When the evidence has information that you cannot dispute, then the reading starts to have real power, real meaning and promotes trust in the psychic or medium.

I don't believe in fortune-telling for this reason, because the power of suggestion is a big part of fortune telling. We can all make things happen. I do believe however in predictions, because to me a prediction is the potential for things to occur. Spirit are aware of what we are doing in our daily lives, therefore they can see people making decisions that will affect us and are likely to happen.

For example, when I woke up one morning I just knew that John and I were going to Melbourne — I had no doubt in my mind. At the time John didn't quite believe me as we had made no plans for travel at that time.

My guides would have known that John's supplier had made a decision to take us there, and that this was going to uplift us both. However, we still had the free choice whether to go or not. I do believe that God has given us free will and we need to make our own decisions, with the free will he has given to us all.

Just before I started my formal training through the SNU, Kara had come up with an idea that I should start doing psychic parties, so I asked other psychics in Auckland how they did this. They didn't want to share their ideas with me, so I came up with my own way of doing it; I would often write messages before the psychic party and on arrival I would pass them to people in the group. We would then stop for a break and I would continue with mediumship after this.

When we were in Melbourne I received an email from a lady who had attended one of my psychic parties. She said she had mentioned me on the radio and did I mind and of course I didn't.

On the return trip to New Zealand I couldn't wait to tell my friends about my email. Kara encouraged me to contact this lady to see if I could go on air and it was agreed that I could. I would be coming into the studio to do a psychic party in Tauranga. Kara booked accommodation and off to Tauranga we went. I was so nervous when I went on air, but at the same time I had fun with the whole event. It all went very well.

Soon after this, a well-known broadcaster arrived at my door for a reading. We seemed to get on very well. As she was leaving she said to me, 'I should get you on More FM and see if we can get you a segment.' My heart skipped a beat but of course I agreed to do it. Not long after this I was in the studio giving readings to the DJs Hayley, Stu and Marc as well as live readings for people phoning in. They referred to my readings as 'snap predictions' and it was a lot of fun.

When John heard that I was giving a reading to Marc Ellis he couldn't stop laughing as he knew I wouldn't know anything about him because of my lack of interest in the news. Here I was telling Marc he was not only good at sport but he was also an entrepreneur and had an excellent future ahead of him! John commented to me later, 'I know what you were giving was spot on, however most of the people who were listening would have thought that of course you already knew all that!'

When the first royal baby was about to be born, I was dreading being asked about the baby's gender. On the way to the radio station a car drove passed with 'coy boy' on the number plate and I knew the baby would be a boy. Thankfully the baby was born before I arrived at the studio so I didn't have to predict the baby's gender in the end. They did ask me what the name of the royal baby is going to be. My guides must have been protecting me that day because I kept on hearing a 'J' or 'G' sound, so when I was asked I was able to say it is like 'J or G' and I pronounced it 'Gi'. Then Marc said 'George' and I said 'Yes, that's it,' and thankfully this was indeed correct.

One morning on air, Marc had a thing about a pumpkin he had been growing in the studio, lovingly attending to every day. When he arrived at work and found that his pumpkin had died he was pretty upset. In fact, he said, 'Someone has murdered my pumpkin! Who is it, Kerry-Marie?' I described a young lady and her name, and they knew who it was. I felt terrible for this poor girl, who was cringing away in the next office. However, I soon learnt not to take radio too seriously — it was a lot of fun and the people I worked with were great. They treated me very well.

I began to be invited into other radio stations; I seemed to receive psychic messages easily, as if the radio frequency helped my psychic ability. Often staff would take me off to side rooms and ask me to give them a mini reading while I was there. On one occasion I gave a reading to a DJ and described her next new love who was from Australia, and indeed that's exactly what happened. I did not want to come across as a fortune teller; a psychic can only give you potential and you always have to take personal responsibility for your own decisions and actions in life. I knew that doing mediumship on radio could be tricky because there is confirmation needed with mediumship but snappy psychic readings work a lot better with this type of media.

Shortly after this, I had a phone call from TV. I was asked to locate Paul Henry's missing signs, but I convinced myself the request was a hoax. I did not want to be made fun of! However I gave them the benefit of the doubt and agreed to be interviewed in my home. As they were setting up I turned to the young man interviewing me and said, 'I can feel your grandfather in spirit. He is wearing a navy uniform and I feel I can't breathe properly.' He looked at me with his mouth open and said, 'My grandfather was in the Navy and he passed with emphysema.' I then told the interviewer that his grandfather just mentioned the name Mary. He replied, 'That is my mother's name and she is my grandfather's daughter.'

He then went on to tell me about the missing signs. Halfway though the interview I told him that one of the crew would be getting married soon, and the cameraman told me that he had been talking on the way there about how he was going to propose to his girlfriend. The whole thing about the missing signs seemed a bit silly, however I did say one of the signs would be returned at Christmas time and, lo and behold, it was indeed dropped off somewhere right over the Christmas period.

Soon after this time I was contacted by *Woman's Day*. I was asked to give a reading to a journalist and I was rather nervous; however when the crew arrived I felt immediately at home with them all. I started the reading and gave information to the journalist, who was very emotional about the beautiful evidence that came through from someone dear to her. I enjoyed the whole experience, especially that they did my hair and make-up! As I've said before, I adore my spiritual work but I have such a passion for fashion and beauty as well. Since I was a child I have loved the feminine side of life, but this was squashed completely as I grew up. What gets in the way of breaking free is fear of expressing yourself and the judgement you may receive from others.

I set off on my journey to become educated under the Spiritual National Union, and was sent information and assigned a tutor who would be marking my essays. I thought I might already know all the course content, but as time went on I discovered I had so much more to learn. I submitted my first three essays thinking I would fly through only, to find out a few weeks later I had failed two out of the three! I was so disappointed with myself, but I picked up the pieces and resubmitted my essays, and passed. Anything worthwhile is never easy.

I had applied to be a wedding celebrant as a client had asked me to officiate her wedding. It's quite a challenge to become a wedding celebrant in New Zealand. After my first submission I was asked to give more evidence of the area I was representing and, to prove it existed, I needed testimonials. I approached many people in the spiritual arena and managed to send in 50 testimonials proving the spiritual community that I represented existed, and there were people in need of a celebrant like myself. Not long after this I was interviewed and granted registration as a marriage celebrant in New Zealand. I came across the School of Celebrant Studies and decided to do various courses, meeting some lovely people along the way.

When I attended celebrant school, I had a feeling of coming home. It felt like I was meeting real people who had a beautiful depth to them. There were two significant things that came out of these courses for me. Firstly, as a medium I was trying to fix people's grief for them and tell them, 'It's OK because their spirit is still here and you haven't lost them.' As much as my heart had been in the right place with this message, I wasn't acknowledging the huge physical pain that comes when someone passes over. It was not my job to fix it, but I was there to respect it and to be there to hold people in their space of grief. This deeper understanding of grief changed my mediumship significantly and I became a more compassionate and understanding medium because of it.

The other thing that occurred was I was now faced with acknowledging my own personal grief that I had locked away for many years. I felt so guilty about my own mothering skills. As a result of my grief, I think, I did not always feel connected to my children. Over a short few years, my father passed, my marriage had broken up, and the two weddings that I had planned with Daniel had been cancelled. The pain of the sexual abuse that I had suffered also came out over this time. I was going through what is known as not only grief but transition; I was going through the motions of life but not really engaging in it. I did my best as a mother but I was not always able to be there for my children as I should have been. The worst thing was, although I knew that I was not functioning properly, instead of giving myself a break, I beat up on myself.

One morning on the way to my celebrant course, deep sobs of release rose up inside me, as I realised I had been carrying the burden of not forgiving myself for years. I had been going through a lot of grief, and what I had been feeling was normal. Society does not often recognise grief or transition, and people often feel guilty because they don't feel that they are really living, only existing. I really do believe if we all understood grief and allowed it to be a part of our lives, then we would all deal with it a lot better than 'just getting over it'. If the process is allowed and accepted then we would work through things much more easily.

Through this journey and celebrant training I was able to forgive a lot of things about myself. It was part of breaking free of the chains of guilt and inner pain that I had carried for so many years. It was like a weight had been taken off my shoulders and I was set free to fly once more. I had not been the perfect mother but I had been the best mother that I could possibly be at the time.

Around this time my business had started to grow. Kara had told me in a reading that a special spiritual lady who had been part of my meditation circle would help me when it came to accounts as I was not particularly good at this part of the business. I accepted that attention to detail was simply not my strength, I had more of a creative personality. Annie suddenly appeared as my earth angel, to help me along this side of my life. As Kara had told me, she had been part of our circle. Spirit send the right people to us at the right time.

I knew I had found my passion. I receive immense joy from working with the spirit world. They give so much healing to the whole world around us, and I feel very privileged. I know I am meant to be doing this work, I am forever overwhelmed and overjoyed with the experiences that I have and the evidence that they bring through, not just to me but many other mediums too, to bring hope, peace and comfort to the bereaved.

Not only did I learn about mediumship and communicating with the spirit world, I also learnt about the healing part of this work. There have been some miracles with the healing work I have done with spirit over my lifetime, such as when a person who had a terrible back injury from an accident many years before found that after healing his back had come right and the pain had disappeared.

As a Spiritualist the question of reincarnation often comes up. Does this really exist? I am pleased to say that the SNU have said that it is up to the individual to decide whether this is true or not. I firmly do believe in past lives and reincarnation, due largely to my healing work. At one point I was doing a healing on a gentleman, I was shown that he had been a drunken sailor in a past life, that he had brought alcoholism with him into this life and that he had managed to get over it in this lifetime,. After his healing he told me this was indeed true.

As time progressed I worked my way through the training offered through the Spiritualist National Union and eventually received three certificates for public speaking, demonstration of mediumship and private sittings. When I went to England to sit my Certificate of Recognition from the Spiritualist National Union, the most challenging situation for me was giving a private sitting with three members of the board in the same room, listening to me give correct evidence of their passed loved ones to the sitter. I knew that accuracy was of prime importance. I had to trust spirit fully when doing this and they must have been working with me the whole time. My intention is to keep developing as a medium and I know we never stop learning.

# *Evidence*

I have mentioned how importance evidence is because the evidence provides comfort for people who have lost a loved one by reassuring them that what they are hearing is real. It is exciting to know there is a spiritual world and it makes everything have meaning and come alive.

The spirit world often knows what we are doing in our daily lives, therefore they can see people making decisions that will affect them and they can support us with this. However it is important that we take personal responsibility for our own decisions in life.

At one time when I was at the Arthur Findlay College, a medium brought my mother through at the Sanctuary. The medium mentioned that she had been around my brother, who has not been well. I could not take this evidence until I returned to stay with my son in Putney along with his partner and my grandson, when I received the very sad news that my darling brother Steven had been diagnosed with cancer. I knew then what the message had meant.

Steven gracefully tried to fight his cancer, he had a huge faith in God and in the power of healing and through his own

Catholic faith he did his best to overcome his illness. Sadly it was his time to go to heaven and we were all distraught at losing our darling loved one. His wife Priscilla was amazing when she nursed him. We were happy that he could give his daughter away at her wedding from his wheelchair and attend both my sons' weddings. He had a quiet determination about him and a few days before he passed he went on a fishing trip in his wheelchair with his family and caught a few snapper. I happened to be visiting as he was going into a coma, and he said 'Hello Kerry'. I felt so touched by this.

That evening I didn't want to leave my brother but respected that Priscilla and his children all wanted to be with him. At about 2.30am I woke with terrible pain around my abdominal area. I tried to wake John up but he was sleeping heavily. Our bedroom door opened and shortly after Priscilla phoned to say that Steven had passed over. Was that my brother giving me his pain, so he could pass? Did his spirit open the door to say goodbye? I can never really say but it did seem a big coincidence. I was so sad to say goodbye to my darling brother, who was always so kind and gentle with me.

## Limiting beliefs

When developing as a medium I became more and more aware of my inner struggles, my limiting beliefs and conditioning as a child. In order to break free I had to deal with my limiting beliefs, there was no other way. One of the limiting beliefs I had when I first started my mediumship, which I still carry with me a little bit, was that I felt I had to be perfect as a person and also with the information I deliver. Fortunately I was able to attend a Doreen Virtue Angel Intuitive Course on a cruise ship and had a lovely time. John was able to come with me as the course was only for a couple of hours most days. We had a lot of fun cruising around the Pacific together, it was a wonderful experience. One of the things I remember from this course was how Doreen spoke about 'the healed healer', and how when people start doing this kind of work, they think they need to be perfect. I knew this applied to me.

Earlier on in my mediumship, when I turned up at my first course many years ago, I dressed up as a hippy because I had this belief that people who did this sort of work were like that. Obviously part of that limiting belief was still with me. I did meet people who did this sort of work who were very *'au naturel'*. I started to feel guilty because I learnt very early on that I cannot be vegetarian as my body needs to be nourished by a variety of foods. Also I sometimes enjoyed a lovely glass of bubbles or red wine, and in the morning I enjoy drinking coffee. Even though I love being healthy and enjoy fitness, I really did not want to get into watching every single thing I ate and how I lived. To me part of being free is to believe that life is for living, but I had some sort of limiting belief about having to be perfect. Feeling guilty about having to be perfect was holding me back from progressing forward.

I also noticed that some of the people who did this sort of work looked very professional and well-presented, and some of them were very alternative-looking. I started to question the fact that I adored beauty and fashion. It makes\ me feel great about being a woman, it makes my heart sing and it is a form of creative expression. In fact with the work I do with helping others I find that activities like having my hair done is my therapy to give me the strength to go on. At the same time part of me felt guilty about this, there seemed to be many spiritual people who talked about the physical only being the physical, they felt it is all about developing our spiritual selves and anything else is superficial. This made me very torn and confused about who I am.

One morning at the spiritual college I felt quite down. I felt torn because I told myself that it was shallow to think about such things with all the poor and sick people in the world. Elizabeth came in around me so strongly at this point, it was like she was wrapping her wings around me (I have often wondered if she is my guide or if she is my guardian angel). Her energy is so soft, gentle and feminine, I can almost smell her freshness when she is around. Suddenly I felt calm and she said to me, 'You are here to be you, to shine and be beautiful on the inside and the outside. Now let it be and I will bring the right people into your life to help you.'

Not long after my return to New Zealand I phoned my friend Paula. She was so excited to hear from me because she told me she had a vivid dream about me contacting her the night before. Paula was very positive and encouraged me on my spiritual path and supported me when I decided to put on shows. Preparation is key for any public presentation and when I am getting ready for a show, I usually meditate in the morning and take myself away from people in the afternoon, so I can attune myself to the spirit world. When you speak in front of people presentation is very important and, just as Elizabeth had promised, Paula was the one who dealt with things like doing my hair and make-up so I could focus on connecting with the spirit world and my guides. She gave me a feeling of peace, strength and confidence.

Along with this, I met a life coach who taught me all about the law of attraction, and made me aware of the effects of limiting beliefs. I knew it was my limiting beliefs that were holding me back from breaking free. She also pointed out how I needed to take personal responsibility for my life, that I could not blame anyone else for where I am at or where I am heading. To set myself free I knew I had to go through a lot of healing within myself. This was a process that took many years and with patience and perseverance I started to get there.

Meanwhile I met Mary, an incredible psychic lady who gave me strength through her wonderful spiritual insight. She was older than me, and soon became like a mother figure in my life. I found her so positive and uplifting. She encouraged me to embrace the feminine, the expressive and creative side of who I was, to enjoy it and that it is OK to just be who you really are.

I knew that I needed the freedom to fly, to say goodbye to what had pinned me down in the past with all the conditioning and expectations of other people. People are often fearful of going to psychics because they feel they are putting their lives into the hands of someone else. I understand perfectly how this is for people and I have been both uplifted and hurt by psychics and mediums in the past. One piece of advice I can give you is whatever is given to you needs to sit right with you. If it doesn't, then your own heart and soul will tell you what is right and what is wrong.

Along with this I found the art of forgiveness is not just for those that had hurt me in the past but also for how I had hurt myself and yes, unintentionally hurt those around me. To carry bitterness or anger in your heart means you are only hurting yourself. By forgiving those who hurt you, you are able to let the burden of hurt go, releasing it from your mind. One of the hardest things to do I believe is to actually forgive yourself, to let go of the things you may have done wrong in life and to become aware that often the best way to learn is by the mistakes we make along the journey of life. By taking personal responsibility for our own choices and actions, we are able to forgive not only others but most importantly ourselves.

During my development and learning I became part of what is known as Spiritual National Union International (SNUI), a division of the SNU. It gives people throughout the world the opportunity to learn about mediumship and spiritualism online. Frequently SNUI holds divine services where there is healing, spiritual philosophy and demonstration of mediumship. I will never forget this particular morning when I was in a service and my father came through a medium. He gave me a message that has always sat with me: 'Everyone has opinions, it does not mean their opinion is right, it is just their opinion. What is right for them may not be right for you. You are letting others' opinions affect you too much, but it's not reality or fact, it's just an opinion.

Live your life the way you choose to.' When you are a recipient you know if the message is correct. As soon as I heard this message I had an amazing feeling of peace go through me.

It takes years to break free of conditioning and limiting beliefs that we have all been brought up with. I know with the support of people around me that I am learning to break free, so I can be there to help people be who they are meant to be. I am like the butterfly breaking free from a chrysalis that had held me encased for so many years. Through the support of God, my spirit helpers, the angels and all the wonderful people here on earth that have been sent to help me on my journey, I have learnt that life is to be lived, enjoyed and celebrated.

It has been very hard for me to let go of my Catholic faith. It had become such a big part of me and even though there are some things about my original faith I really do not agree with, there are amazing parts to it as well. I still respect some of the beliefs and rituals, and I can see the similarities between both faiths I have been part of. I went with my own knowing that there are many roads to follow, we are not all the same and that God to me is not a judging God. The God I know is a creative energy that is gentle, caring and compassionate, and more loving than words could ever describe. One could say a tremendous, unconditional, eternal, loving force.

God is in all of us. We all come from a loving, creative force that urges us to be the best possible being we can be. Through life experiences we can feel trapped and lost. This creative force urges us to break free from the restraints that hold us back from progressing forward to be who we are meant to be. We are eternal souls, learning and evolving with endless possibilities not only before us but inside of us.

If you feel pinned down, trapped and lost, ask the higher source that you believe in to help you break free, to find who you truly are, what you are here for. Before long miracles will start to occur as you discover new situations. Opportunities will manifest in your life, setting you on your path to your own personal freedom. Your creativity, your personal expression of who you truly are and what you are here for will then become clear. You will be led to where you need to be when you fly free with the winds of love beneath your wings.

# Demonstration of mediumship

When I began to develop as a medium I was very happy to do one on one sittings with people, but I never imagined I would ever demonstrate on a platform publically.

After the passing of my mother and Amanda's show, I was being guided to do more and more public demonstrations, which at first I did not find easy.

There was one demonstration that I did in a spiritual church that changed my perception on all of this. The local spiritualist church asked me to be the medium that Sunday evening and I went into a complete panic, so decided I really needed to calmly prepare myself. Then a miracle occurred.

Driving to the church I decided to call into my husband's business and do a quick meditation in my office. Within a very short time a lady joined me and she told me very clearly, 'I am still a regular visitor to my church and when I was here on earth I would come and sit on the left-hand side of the church at the front next to the aisle'. When I finished the meditation I felt quite spacey like I really had gone into an altered state.

On arrival at the church I felt calmer than I had at previous demonstrations and when I took the platform this lovely lady who had previously been with me blended with my aura so I could feel her even more strongly than before. I introduced this strong woman who used to visit the church every Sunday to the congregation and pointed to the seat where she used to sit. She was insistent that I call her a mother and a grandmother, then the congregation started laughing at me. This made me feel really unsure but I kept on going with the information she was giving me. She took me to my stomach area and I knew that she had passed with a cancerous condition relating to this area.

The evidence that was coming through just seemed to flow through me and was confirmed by the lady sitting at the front. She then told me that this was her grandmother and that she was a regular visitor to the church, and that she would always sit in the particular chair I was pointing to and that is why everyone was laughing at me as they all knew her. At one point I mentioned something that was always next to her when she was in hospital. One of the family members called out that it was the morphine pump but I shook my head as she was showing me something far more relevant than this. In my mind's eye I could see so clearly a small black Bible. Her granddaughter gasped as she realised that this was her very special Bible that she would take everywhere with her. It was like this very spiritual lady who had now passed to the spirit world could see my potential, and decided to work with me not only to bring through evidence and comfort to her family but also to install more confidence in me as a medium.

From the visit of this very special Maori lady my demonstrations took off as I knew I had nothing to be afraid of, and that the beautiful presence of spirit and the love they have for those on the earth plane was the most important thing. On arrival home I burst into tears, realising once again how real all this work was, that my purpose and job here on earth was to be the best medium

I could be to bring love, peace, comfort, hope and healing through from the world of spirit to those living here on earth.

Not long after this service I was asked to demonstrate again at another church and something very similar occurred. This time just before the service I decided to have a quick meditation in the car and I heard the voice of a spirit tell me her name was Gwen. She had fallen down some stairs and died in October. The information was so specific and detailed that when I went to demonstrate I could feel the lady blending with me so strongly that I knew where she was taking me in the room. Within a short time her nephew enthusiastically raised his hand as I described his aunty, her white spotted dog and also gave his name, a description of her loving yet practical personality, along with her first name, month of passing and lastly her surname. There were gasps in the audience as the details were given, but more comforting than that was the joyful expression on her nephew's face, almost like he was relieved and at peace. Once more the power of mediumship had touched another soul.

When someone younger passes to the spirit world it is very hard for the family left behind as there are very often unanswered questions. One evening at church with a healing session underway, I felt myself going into a slightly altered state as spirit started to connect with my energy. It was almost as if they were surrounding my head. Stepping into my aura was a young woman who was both showing herself and speaking to me. At the time I could feel her urgency and that she wanted to make peace with someone in the audience. She was urging me to go towards the bottom right hand side of the church.

When the time came to demonstrate this young lady connected with me even more strongly and I pointed to the area she was insistent I go to. At first I had no idea what she was going to communicate so I just went with it. Once again the evidence she gave me was very detailed and specific, so I started to describe her along with her cancerous condition, that she loved fashion, was fussy with her hair, involved in the media and television, and that she was with her five-year-old daughter in the spirit world. Everyone just stared back at me and no hands were raised so I repeated the information again pointing to the area she was taking me as she was very determined to come through.

Very sheepishly a lady put up her hand. She had formed a relationship with the spirit lady's husband and was taking care of her children for her. From the feeling and peace of the spirit I could sense that there were no hard feelings, she wanted to give her a sense of peace and to thank her for taking care of her children, and she wanted to let her husband know that she was safely with their daughter in the spirit world. Later on the lady in the audience contacted me to thank me so much for this message and how much peace and comfort she had received from it. Her partner was also at peace knowing that his daughter was safe with her mother in heaven.

Occasionally I can feel a bit alarmed or surprised when I go to demonstrate because, as my father used to say, 'it takes all types to make a world'. One evening this was definitely the case. Once again through the healing session I could feel the presence of spirit drawing closer to me and a bit of an unruly man started to push his way forward so I told him to step back, that he wasn't going first (as that is what he wanted) and that he needed to be patient. Initially I was a bit hesitant but trusted that the spirit world always show themselves as they were to give evidence and that they always come with love. He took me aback when he showed me that he was a gang member holding a knife and I sensed he got up to all types of criminal activity in his life as well as being involved heavily with drugs.

Most times I demonstrate there is one particular spirit that is stronger and more evidential with their information than others and this was the case that particular evening. He showed me exactly where he wanted to go and I could see his family sitting next to each other with smiles on their faces as their father came through with all sorts of interesting information, not the type I was used to! Nevertheless the healing and love was still there and he wanted them to live more honest, responsible lives than the one he had lived. Their dad only wanted the very best for his family and it was his soul's love that was coming through.

# 30

## *The power of mediumship*

One thing I have learnt over the years and from breaking free from restrictions of conditioning, limiting beliefs and doubts is that the power of mediumship is truly incredible.

Our own soul and spirit is connected to a creative power much larger than our own and there is so much more than we know or can understand here on earth.

Growing up in a strict religious family gave me some knowledge of spirituality, however it restricted me from growing and learning more. It was so confusing for me as a young child seeing, hearing and sensing spirit all around me and not understanding what was actually happening.

Looking back I can see that there was a plan for my life. All my experiences, both good and bad, led me to where I am today. Never would I have thought that I would be a full-time working medium when I think of the family I was born into. In fact it would seem that nothing would be more unlikely. So what led me here?

Deep down inside, my soul knew I would be here to empower and assist people with their lives. From a young age I was interested in spiritual topics and having spiritual experiences. Through difficulties and personal pain, I was able to grow and heal to follow the guiding light of spirit to fulfill my life purpose.

There are so many different types of mediumship; just like most things in life they need to be explored on a deeper level to fully understand how it all works. The power of mediumship will always fascinate me and I see it as a wondrous gift that transforms your own life as well as others.

From my own experience if I had not hit rock bottom in my mid-thirties I would never have turned to a psychic for help. The fact that my father's spirit came through a medium was truly amazing and both healed and transformed my life forever.

Often mediums have difficult lives and this is so they can help and understand others. If I had not experienced my father's spirit all those years ago, I feel I would still have unresolved grief, and my father would not have been able to make peace with me for the healing of his own spirit. Not only that, it allowed me to process his loss, face myself honestly and seek the help that I so needed at that time. I would not like to think where I would be now if I had not been fortunate to visit that first medium.

Through my own experience of seeing a medium I was put on the path to become the medium I was born to be. It was through this process that I was set free.

Now mediumship that transforms and heals others is, to me, the most precious gift of all.

When a mother comes to vist me because of the sudden death of her child through a car accident, that poor mother's grief is horrendous. Very often they do not know what to do with it or how to go on with their lives. Even though many tears are shed when their child makes themselves known, they are so relieved when they realise their child is still OK, and that most importantly they will see them again one day.

Another example is the husband who is lost because his

darling wife has suffered, and then passed over with cancer. He does not know how to go on without her, even though he knows she could not stay with him. He is so very relieved to hear from her. He will have a more peaceful sleep after he knows that she is OK and they will be together again.

Many people suffer from guilt when someone has passed and it can be very hard to deal with. In some cases it can be because of the people left behind and they didn't say goodbye, or had an argument with the person before they passed over. Sometimes it could be because the spirit wants to make peace with the people who are still alive.

When contact is made and good evidence is given, it sets both parties free to live their own lives without the guilt and unresolved issues that may be there. Those who have the opportunity to have this spiritual experience are very often transformed forever.

Mediumship is such an important and reverent gift that I treat with the greatest of respect. I am forever thankful for the ability I have with mediumship, to be able to connect with the other world. I know that God has bestowed this gift upon me and I will be forever grateful and honoured that I can do this. Its power is tremendous and it is all because of love that the gift of mediumship comes about in the first place. The love of spirit is so strong that against all odds the spirit world do their best to communicate with their loved ones on earth to let them know that they are OK. They want their loved ones to be happy and at peace and they look forward to seeing you as much as you would love to see them again in the future.

Spirit often comes through with helpful insights and advice for the living. It could be that they are looking at getting a new job, starting a new business or having relationship issues. From my experience their advice is very often valid. They may give you a name of someone who is in need of some support. They never tell you what to do, however the information they pass on is often insightful and comes with love. Free will is important and they respect this. They only want the best for you.

The powerful gift of mediumship has not only set me free, it continues to set many others free as well to live their lives, heal and continue on their journey. I know without a doubt I am being looked after and surrounded by spiritual love.

# 31

## *Michael and Violet*

A few weeks before my first show, a very distressed lady called Violet came to see me. She was obviously grieving but didn't tell me why. A man came through very quickly and strongly; it was her husband giving me his name, Michael. He indicated to me that he had passed very suddenly and it was a shock.

Michael was Violet's soul-mate and best friend. I was able to describe him physically and also that I could see him in my mind's eye wearing a shirt and tie. I was also able tell her that Michael was a very kind, friendly, outgoing man, and that nothing was too much trouble for him when it came to helping people. He was a real gentleman. When he was younger he had a very good job which was connected to military and he wore a uniform (Violet confirmed later he had been in the police). Violet said very little as I continued to say that Michael had a son and daughter, which was correct. He made it clear he'd had a heart attack and gave me the pain of it (it hurt so much I had to ask him to stop). Spirit connects with our auric field and even though it does not affect our physical body the energy can sometimes make you feel like it is.

I then was able to describe him as a very good husband, a handyman who liked to fix things and to keep busy, a gentle giant who was kind to other people. He liked sport, animals especially horses, and had a real sense of humour. He never took himself seriously, and was also open-minded and easy to talk to. The month of August was significant. Michael then went on to pass so much love to her. He said he was around her all the time, and that he would always be just a thought away. Michael was watching her deal with legal papers and other difficulties, and wanted this to turn out well for all concerned. He was very proud of her. He mentioned a new baby in the family and that he watches over her (a new grandchild had been born a few weeks before he passed). Near the end of the reading he mentioned a plant which I could see purple in and presumed it was a purple flower he was showing me. Little did I know at the time how crucial this information was to be.

Michael kept saying how much he cared for her, how sorry he was that he had left and how much it hurt.

Violet then said she was nervous about the reading and didn't want to trust too much as she had been with great hope to another medium previously. The other medium had not achieved a strong link with Michael. Even though the medium thought she was doing a good job, to Violet it seemed she had gone to lengths describing another spirit whom she did not know and all the pointers were wrong. Violet explained that even though the medium did her best, it ended up being completely devastating for her and she returned home in a very low state.

While she was sitting at home lost in despair thinking that there was no point in her continuing to live, she found herself looking at a plain green plant on the coffee table. The plant developed a lavender glow which flickered and stayed for some time, long enough for her to realise it wasn't an imagined flash of light, but a message for her. She had neither real belief in the spirit world, nor any concept of life after death, but after that moment she decided to try again. That is why she came to me.

I was pleased when she explained this background. She gave me his photo from the funeral sheet, and the photo showed him wearing the shirt and tie I described earlier. I explained that sometimes all I see is a quick vision in my mind and this was one he had shown me. She had been confused when I described Michael's outfit as he was normally in scruffy work clothes, generally wearing shorts along with boots, but the suit now made complete sense.

She asked me if his spirit had been at the funeral as she had tried the best she could. She didn't give me any further details though. This is difficult as the connection is not like a phone call with chat back and forth, but I went back to his spirit. He said he was there, and described the venue. He loved the music and gave me an arm movement which described bagpipes, the purple-coloured flowers on the coffin (there were bunches of lavender), and a light brown coffin with a white lining. He gave me that the place was special to him (it was in the barn at his home), he showed me an older building, with steps leading into a light greenish-coloured square building. It was a happy place for him surrounded by trees. He also said that someone was late for the funeral, and that the new baby was also there. Violet confirmed that this was all correct and gave her a sense of peace and hope to know that he really was present and his spirit continued to live on.

After our first session I was not convinced that I had satisfied Violet enough, even though I had brought through very good evidence and done my best for her. At this time a friend of mine who also had a wonderful psychic gift told me that she felt there had been a lady who had come to see me and that I thought she was not satisfied with me, but she would listen to the reading and be one of my greatest supporters. Looking back I am positive this was Michael's spirit giving this information to my friend to pass onto me.

In the next reading he went back to the funeral again and I sang a song he gave me — 'Love, Love, Love' by the Beatles. Violet said she had chosen that piece of music for his funeral ceremony when the hearse was leaving with his coffin. When she realised this the tears began to flow.

Violet came back for regular readings and it felt like she was having chats with her darling husband Michael each time. Even though she was convinced that her husband's spirit lived on, she felt he did not need to always give her evidence of his life on earth any more. He still continued to do, describing many events occurring in her life. Violet found this to be of great comfort.

Often at our sessions Michael would mention that Violet would need to shift into a new home. She did not want to take this information on as she was happy in her current residence with all of Michael's memories around her. However Michael was very insistent about this, like he was preparing her.

One day Violet was given the news she didn't want to hear. She had to suddenly leave the house that they had lived in and move somewhere else, for reasons beyond her control. Michael was clear in the reading that she had to move, it was a good thing, he would definitely be there and then he described the house she was to buy: white, wooden, with a stream in the garden of lavender and roses, a cockerel was there and it was on a sort of hill with paddocks around. There was a helicopter nearby. Well, she found exactly that house and moved in and was happy to be there. Michael now describes the things she has been doing there, even to the detail of watching her manage the drill and put in door stops!

Other spirits who were important to Violet would come through, and all gave her the comfort and strength to go on and recover through the grief and sadness, knowing that she had their love and support.

All this opened up Violet's awareness of the spirit world and she went on developing her own spiritual sensitivity through my courses and workshops. Violet now has written records on the readings and information that comes through from Michael and has found the whole experience totally fascinating. She continues to tell many people about the joy and comfort she receives from her darling husband, who still continues to console her from the spirit world. She encourages many people to seek a medium when they are going through times of grief from loss.

Little did Violet know that through her own sadness she would help others. She has also started to develop as a medium, a gift that she never knew she had. Violet attends many of my workshops that assist in the development of other mediums as well as public demonstrations and shows. As my friend had said, she is indeed one of my biggest supporters.

# 32

## Transformation through the power of spirit

One afternoon I was chatting to Paula as she was doing my hair. We were discussing some of my shows where she had watched me from the audience. She was able to look at the whole thing from a completely different perspective.

She said, 'Kerry-Marie, I don't know how to tell you this, but when you stand up in front of people when you are demonstrating, it's like you become a completely different person. I can't really explain it, you seem more confident, calm and at peace. It's like you have transformed into a beautiful butterfly.'

At first I didn't know quite how to take her words. I knew they were positive, uplifting and encouraging but at the same time I could not quite understand how she could see me as a different person, because from my point of view I was just being Kerry-Marie. I then asked myself, what is transformation all about?

The answer started to become quite clear. Transformation is the power of spirit blending with my energy to make me appear different to how my friends and people see me on a day-to-day basis. When a medium opens up her energy and her auric field to blend with the power of spirit, something very magical takes place.

We are all spirit contained in a physical body, and within our spirit is our soul. Our soul is our guiding voice and knows what is right and wrong for us. When we go within to who we truly are, we can become a different person. Something about it gives us a sense of peace and calmness. As a medium when I open up my own soul and spirit to blend with the spirit world, my vibration is raised to meet with them. It truly is a beautiful, magical experience. One could even say it is a miracle.

The power of spirit is not only a huge intelligence, it is full of love, peace and hope. When my own spirit blends with the spirit world a beautiful transformation occurs as I become one with them. I can see that from an outsider's point of view I could come across as a completely different person.

Often when I have blended well with the spirit world, and particularly when I am describing an individual, it is almost like I become them. Suddenly I may want to kick up my heels and dance, ride a bike or start to draw, sing a song or play a musical instrument.

We all have a variety of emotions which at times can be quite strong. This is the same with the spirit world. In a demonstration or a private sitting, sometimes I have to hold back the tears because the emotions coming from the spirit and blending with my energy can be quite powerful. In a private situation, at times though I have allowed some tears to flow. If this occurs the sitter understands that these tears of love are coming through from spirit as a recognition of their love for them.

It was interesting that Paula had described me as a beautiful butterfly, as this was a theme that started to present itself to me. When I look back over my life and the restrictions that had occurred from a variety of experiences, I can see that both the power of spirit and my own soul have been guiding me to break free of the shackles that had previously held me down and prevented me from moving forward.

Many of us have challenges and obstacles to overcome in life. It can be easy to blame others for this, however I believe if we take personal responsibility for ourselves, search within our own inner being and let our souls speak to us, we can find perfect peace and know what we are here for.

Fortunately I have been blessed with the sacred gift of mediumship. By allowing my soul to be my guiding light, along with the power of spirit at times I can transform into the beautiful butterfly and break free from the past and live my life purpose.

Of course I am human and living an earthly experience with all the ups, downs and challenges like everyone else. Saying that, when I am working with spirit and connecting with their vibration I feel like I am truly being who I am meant to be. The only way I have been able to achieve this has been through my own personal development, and willingness to learn and grow over time.

One of my biggest learning curves has been to forgive and love those who have hurt me. This can be an ongoing process for many of us. At the same time, forgiveness can set you free from the burdens of the past so you can fly and transform into who you truly are and what you are here for.

My own soul and spirit has guided me to break free.

# *If I Had Wings*

The sky full of sky stuff; the forests of trees
The birds and the insects; the slugs with no knees
You are more precious than all of these things
I would fly to you if I had wings

The sea full of sea things; the beaches with sand
The dolphins and fishes; the crustaceans
You are more precious than all of these things
I would swim to you if I had fins

The sky full of sky stuff; the forests of trees
The birds and the insects; the slugs with no knees
You are more precious than all of these things
I would fly to you if I had wings
I would fly to you if I had wings

© Bos O'Sullivan 2011

# With gratitude

I would like to thank Kerry-Marie for:

- Being brave enough to come out with her gift, withstanding critics and naysayers.
- Caring enough about others with their grief to the point of draining herself physically and mentally.
- Always being uplifting to others even though dealing with difficulties herself.
- Being so patient with people who don't want to believe in spirit and eventually being able to give clear evidence and personal messages, so they are then able to take comfort from the knowledge that spirit is there for them, caring and helping from their other world.
- Being humble and still full of wonder at the amazing world of spirit.
- Taking the time to teach many to develop their own spirituality and psychic and mediumship abilities.
- Helping me gently through a devastating time and showing me so clearly that I am not alone, I am still loved and supported and we will be together again one day in that other world that really does exist.

Tina

Kerry-Marie is a wonderfully gifted medium.

I met Kerry-Marie seven years ago, and her first reading for me was life-changing. She connected with many of my relatives and friends in spirit, plus two beloved pets.

I was so impressed with her accuracy, visual detail, and the love that came through from spirit. Since then, I have had many more readings and healings from Kerry-Marie. I feel so blessed to know that our lives are indeed eternal.

Kerry-Marie is a very special lady, an Earth Angel with a big heart.

I feel privileged to call her my friend.

Karen Baker


I first met Kerry-Marie not long after my darling husband passed away. A mutual friend recommended that I visit Kerry-Marie as I was finding it hard to come to terms with my loss.

As soon as I met Kerry-Marie I immediately felt her compassion, love and understanding. Straight away I felt at ease, relaxed and able to trust her with my emotions and grief.

My husband and I were so close — soul mates. I knew that the experiences I'd had since he passed were his presence, but I was not totally sure. I had never experienced these things before — lights turning on in the middle of the night, music randomly playing on my phone. Right from my first reading Kerry-Marie confirmed that he was around me and our children all the time. There were so many situations that Kerry-Marie told me about that you could only know if you were actually there — providing proof that my husband was communicating with me.

It has been such a blessing to me and our children knowing that our 'Boy' is still with us, loving and guiding us. It has helped us to carry on and move in to the future.

Kerry-Marie has made this possible.

Kerry-Marie, you are an angel, thank you.

Tracy

# Acknowledgements

I wish to say thank you to:

- My wonderful husband, John Callander, who has supported me throughout writing this book. Thanks also to my three children, stepchildren and their partners, and also to all my grandchildren for their love that I have found so uplifting over this time.
- My loving and amazing friends, you know who you are and how much support and encouragement you have given with my journey. Thank you so very much.
- My mother, even though I had a difficult relationship with her in the early years of my life. As a young child I didn't really understand why she was the way she was, but in later years she became my best friend, confidante and rock, and I recognized her heart of gold.
- My amazing father, who was full of love and warmth during my life. Because of his spirit coming through a medium to speak to me at age 35, I was able to acknowledge my abilities and lead my true life as a spiritual medium. It showed me how healing mediumship truly is, and enabled me to follow the journey through with his spirit close to me.
- To the professional people who helped me with this book, for all your support, encouragement, strength and the

sharing of your experience and wisdom, especially Leanne Kidd, Lianne Reidy, Michelle Charles, Anne Mandeno and Tracey Wogan for helping me with the editing process and the support and time you gave me, and Andre Budel and Simon Llewellyn for their wonderful cover photos.

Printed in the United States
By Bookmasters